C.R.I.C.K.E.T.

DAN LIEBKE

CONTENTS

ON BOWLERS AND SPORTSMANSHIP

FEATURING AN AUSTRALIAN CRICKET CAPTAIN

The oafish ineptitude of my bowling attack has always, and will always, appal me. I feel physically ill every time I see their disgusting, hairy, perspiration-drenched bodies, pounding in with all the gracelessness of a sex-starved buffalo to deliver yet another of their wayward projectiles at the batter. Their stain-riddled trousers, their preposterous facial hair, their needy pleas for reassurance that they're bowling well even when they decidedly are not. I despise them all, from Mitchell to Nathan to Mitchell to Douglas to Mitchell.

No matter how many runs I amass with clinical, yet stylish, wielding of my Limited Edition Spartan blade, it's impossible to be certain that it's ever enough for these feckless mesomorphs. A century. A double century. A triple century. I surpass these milestones with debonair aplomb, pausing only to acknowledge the palpable adoration of the crowd, mindlessly cheering in worship. They *adore* me. I am their God, and I deign to bestow upon these pitiable sheep an iota of meaning for their joyless lives with nothing more than a casual salute of my insatiable bat.

The only thing preventing me from scoring a quadruple century or more is my own keen determination to ensure there's sufficient time left in the match for the talentless cavemen upon whom I'm criminally forced to rely to take the twenty wickets for a win. If not for the allowances I am forced to make in compensation for their staggering ineptitude, the record books would be overwhelmed by my unfettered talent. There are few things in this universe more certain than that.

And yet, I am cursed with the knowledge of their multitudinous limitations. Their refusal to bowl to my orders. Their ignorance of what it takes to defeat our opponents, no matter how lacking in spirit or talent those foes might be. Their wretched excuses that they've once again injured their knee or their back. Or worse. Sometimes a fast bowler will attempt to start a conversation with me about a 'groin twinge' or their 'grunt muscle'. I will not abide this.

And so I sacrifice my own ambitions for the greater good. I am a modern day Mandela, a leader of men, willing to do whatever it takes to win. And devil take the hysterical critics and their incessant, baseless claims that my single-minded goal of total cricketing domination goes too far.

What these blinkered imbeciles fail to understand is that there is nothing personal to the merciless abuse I inflict on my opponents. A relentless tirade of targeted debasement does not mean that I hate all Indians. Nor all South Africans. Nor even all Englishmen. No, I hate only the ones against whom we are asked to compete. That is, after all, why I so proudly wear the baggy green. (At least, metaphorically. In practice, it is an item of headwear that fails on every functional level, and I refuse to allow it to taint my precisely gelled locks for a millisecond more than is symbolically necessary.)

I am aware that the criticism of me and my team's relentless push for excellence and victory is fuelled by rampant jealousy. I am confronted by such resentment everywhere I turn. I understand why. For others to look at me, with my piercing eyes, striking features and 7.1% body fat, and *not* feel envy would be the more remarkable outcome. Of course the gormless sports writers and the social media snivelers are jealous. Look at what I've accomplished. I'm the captain of the Australian cricket team. The greatest captain of them all.

And that's why I allow my contempt for the critics to pass through me. I am paid to win cricket matches. And that means I am obliged to push the Laws of this game to their very limits. Because to do anything less is tantamount to deliberate underperformance.

Furthermore, my ingrained professionalism requires that not even the Laws of the game limit my actions. For if you don't expect players to run afoul of the Laws then why does one require umpires? The behaviour of me and the team I lead validates the very existence of those insipid ball-counters, whether it be Bradley knocking off a bail and claiming the batter has been bowled, or Cameron scuffing the ball to engender the kind of reverse swing our ineffectual attack need to succeed, or any one of us claiming a catch that might not have, technically, carried.

I will not hesitate to push the Laws of the game as I strive for another earthily aromatic sampling from the golden decanter of victory. And I will not apologise for my ambition. This is a concept which that dimwitted showman Brendon will never understand. But know this: if I get caught in the act, I take it on the chin and never complain. Unless, of course, by mustering an emphatic denial and arguing with the officials, I can browbeat them into being less inclined to challenge me next time. And they *will* hesitate. Because they are weak. Not like me. My will is iron and my determination to destroy all who dare to oppose me through whatever means is necessary must never be in question.

Defy me at your peril. For I will brook no counterarguments. And I will crush you into nothingness until you regret your decision to ever show any semblance of interest in the game of cricket.

You will weep as you depart the scene, your love of the sport crushed beyond repair, and I will laugh at your pain.

Thank you for coming to my MCC Spirit of Cricket Lecture.

THE PAKISTAN GUIDE TO WINNING A TEST

Here's how virtually every other team in world cricket approaches winning a Test match when bowling first:

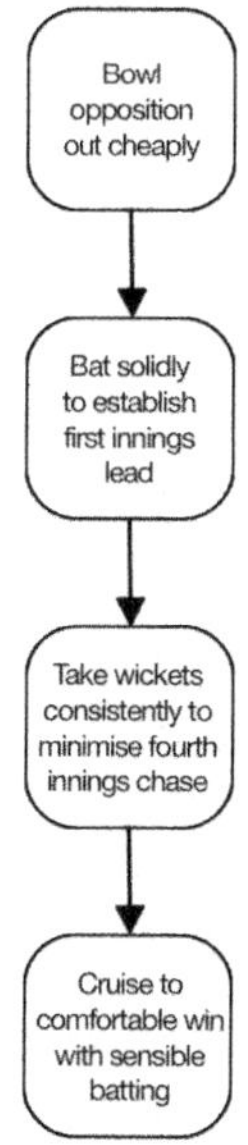

Here's how Pakistan does it:

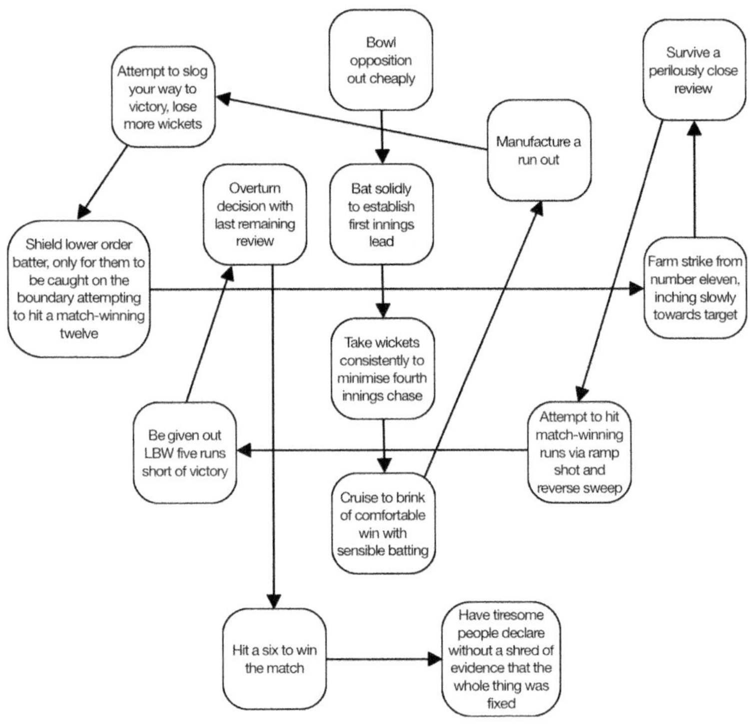

And that's why Pakistan is the greatest cricket team in the world.

SEVEN CRICKET RIDDLES AND LATERAL THINKING PUZZLES

Keep your mind alert and your wits sharp with these classic riddles and lateral thinking puzzles from the Australian cricket team.

QUESTION 1

Glenn Maxwell walks one mile due south, then one mile due east, then one mile due north and arrives back at his starting point. He takes a catch from a bear. What colour was it?

Answer: Red. (Cameron White's nickname is 'Bear'. He played for the Melbourne Renegades, who dress in red. Why this BBL Melbourne local derby was being played at the North Pole, however, remains anybody's guess.)

QUESTION 2

One of the two onfield umpires can only send truthful soft signals. The other can only send soft signals that are lies. A low catch is sent upstairs to the third umpire, who may ask only one further question. How does the third umpire determine if the batter is out?

Answer: Rather than muck about with convoluted questioning of the onfield umpires such as 'if I asked the other umpire what soft signal they'd send, would they say 'out' or 'not out'?', the third umpire instead asks the television broadcasters for a replay of the bowler's front foot, which reveals a no ball. Not out.

QUESTION 3

A tailender has made ten more runs than the score their more senior batting partner had when the partnership began. The more senior partner, meanwhile, has tripled their score. The sum of their two scores is now one hundred runs. How is their partnership broken?

Answer: Let x be the number of runs the more senior batting partner had when the partnership began. The more senior batter now has 3x runs. The tailender has x+10 runs. The total number of runs is therefore 4x+10.

$4x+10 = 100 \rightarrow 4x = 90 \rightarrow x = 22.5$

The tailender is therefore on 32.5 (x+10) and the more senior partner on 67.5 (3x).

As they are only halfway through a run, one of them will be easily run out, ending the partnership in an acrimonious fashion.

QUESTION 4

Which weighs more? A ton of feathers or a ton of bricks?

Answer: It depends who the ton was scored against.

QUESTION 5

A batter on strike needs to transport a fox, a chicken and a sack of grain to the non-striker's end. The batter can, however, only carry one of them with each run. If the batter leaves the fox with the chicken, the fox will eat the chicken. Similarly, if they leave the chicken with the grain, the grain will be eaten. How many runs does the batter need to hit to transport everything to the non-striker's end?

Answer: Zero. Just summon security onto the ground to deal with this ridiculous state of affairs. How in blue blazes did a *fox* get into the ground in the first place? Is it a Fox Cricket mascot of some kind? Sort it out, Cricket Australia.

QUESTION 6

Which Australian cricketer walks on four legs in the morning, two legs in the afternoon, and three legs in the evening?

Answer: An Australian cricketer walking? Grow up.

QUESTION 7

A father and son go to watch the cricket. During the innings break, the son wins a prize to bowl an over to the captain of the Australian cricket team. But before he gets a chance to do so, the captain stops him and say 'I can't face an over from this boy. He's my son.' How is this possible?

Answer: The Australian cricket captain is a woman, you sexist fuck! (Also, she's lying about the boy being her son. She thinks this is a stupid publicity stunt and wants to end it and get her team focused on defending their total of 390 (A Healy 281* (64), B Mooney 100* (56)) from their twenty overs.)

MURDER BY PODCAST!

A TRAGIC DETECTIVE MYSTERY

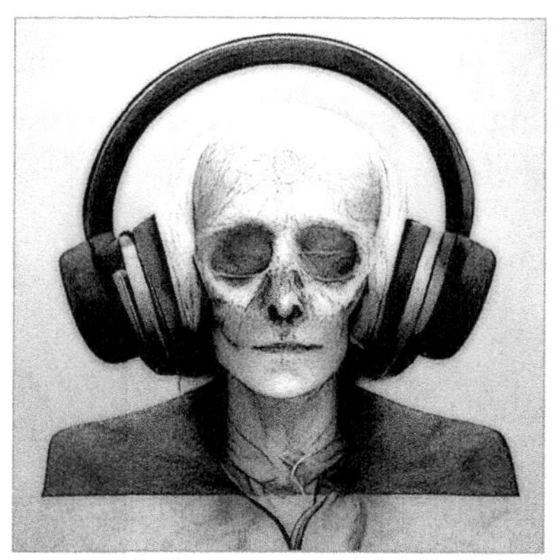

As always, the first drinks break on the first day of the First Test at the Gabba was set aside for Senior Constable Vickers of the Queensland Police Service, a bull of a man consistently sporting facial expressions that suggest he somehow has rocks in his underwear.

I met Vickers at the end of the row and ushered him along to the detective, who had finished totting up his scorecard and was now spraying himself with a fresh layer of sunscreen.

"Senior Constable," said the detective, his voice muffled by the UPF-80 mist that enveloped him.

"Detective," said Vickers, the honorific, as always, an obvious irritant to him.

"How can I help you this Test?"

"Have you heard of The Ornitholocast?" asked Vickers.

"Of course," said the detective, as the fog of sunscreen began to recede. "It was easily the most terrifying new dinosaur in the latest Jurassic Park movie. I shrieked like an England tail-ender facing Mitchell Johnson when it tore that CrossFit trainer in half."

"Uh, no," said Vickers. "I'm talking about Queensland's fourth favourite podcast." He stared quizzically at the detective, who had begun slapping the sunscreen into his exposed flesh. "I take it you haven't heard of it then?"

"Ah," said the detective, between slaps. "No." Then, "What are the first three?"

Vickers consulted his notepad. "According to the latest charts, number three is 'The Prodcast with Buggo and The Crack', in which Queensland's favourite 'prodcasters' poke everyday items with a cattle prod and report back on the results."

Vickers continued. "Number two is 'Murder Me Maybe', a true crime podcast that each week analyses the lyrics of Carly Rae Jepsen's 'Call Me Maybe', searching for evidence of the Canadian singer-songwriter's involvement in unsolved murders."

"And number one?" asked the detective.

"It's still 'QUEENSLANDER!!! with Billy Moore', in which Billy shouts the word 'Queenslander!' over and over for eighty minutes."

"Of course," said the detective, nodding. "And The Ophthalmolocast is fourth, right?"

"The Ornitholocast," corrected Vickers. "It's hosted by Professor Michael Huber, and it discusses, via the medium of birds, the philosophy and practicalities of navigating through all facets of modern society."

"Birds?" said the detective. "Does he talk about Jackson Bird?"

"No."

"Aaron Finch?" tried the detective. "Graeme Swann? Martin Crowe?"

"No," repeated Vickers.

"Robin Smith? Glenn 'Pigeon' McGrath? Joel 'Big Bird' Garner?"

"No, none of those," clarified Vickers, and I could see the detective's interest fade immediately. "He deals solely with actual, feathered birds. It's very popular, and brilliantly made - 'a podcasting tour de force' is how Queensland Podcasts Monthly described it. Huber is already acknowledged as a genuine podcast auteur - the inventor of the hot new aviancast subgenre of podcasting. SportsBet has him at 1.30 to win the 'Best New Podcast' and 'Podcast of the Year' double at the Queensland Expo for Excellence in Podcasting next month."

"Ah yes, the QuEEPers," said the detective. The sunscreen had finally been hammered into his skin, and he was now busily attempting to remove its sun-repellent droplets from his spectacles via his tattered 'Choose Life' T-shirt. "So what seems to be the problem?"

"We believe Huber killed his producer last night," said Vickers. "But we have no idea how."

"This isn't working at all," muttered the detective to himself, finally realising that his T-shirt was covered in the same sunscreen spray he was trying to clean from his glasses. He donned the smudged spectacles and peered through them at Vickers. "Tell me more," he said.

"The producer - a Mr Ed Small - was found dead in his apartment this morning, apparently strangled to death. He was discovered at his desk, with microphone cables wrapped around his throat. His computer had been fried by an electrical surge and there was an open can of sardines on the table beside him. He was still wearing his headphones. There were no signs of forced entry."

"I can picture it vividly," said the detective. "What was the time of death?"

"This is where it gets interesting," said Vickers. "The coroner established the time of death as between 7pm and 8pm."

"That *is* interesting," agreed the detective absently, his gaze carefully monitoring the umpires returning to their officiating positions. "But we need to hurry this along."

"Our problem is that Huber has an alibi for the entire evening. He was in a hotel room recording his latest episode."

"A hotel room?" asked the detective.

"It's part of his process apparently," explained Vickers. "From very early on in his podcasting career, he took to booking a room at The Dead Zone in the city, where he'd lock himself in for the night and record his podcast. We've interviewed the staff there, and Huber checked in at 6pm last night, before checking out this morning at 8am."

"He didn't leave at any point?"

"Not according to the staff. They brought his dinner up at 7:36pm and knocked on the door. He told them he was still podcasting and they should leave it outside the room. One of the hotel reflexologists noticed the food still there at 8:44pm and knocked once more, but he again replied 'still podcasting'. When they returned at 9:33pm the food was gone, and the empty dishes were left outside around 10:51pm."

"Could the staff be covering for him?" asked the detective.

"Unlikely," said Vickers. "He's not popular with the staff. They describe him as rude, demanding and prone to leaving nuts and other food scraps strewn all over the carpet. His only positive quality, according to the owner of the hotel, is that even in the middle of a Brisbane summer, he'll never turn the air conditioning on because he's concerned the noise will impact the recording. He just opens the window instead. Saves the hotel a fortune in electricity apparently."

"Opens the window?" said the detective, watching carefully as the batters returned to the middle. The ball was tossed to the spinner.

"I know what you're thinking," said Vickers. "But his room is three floors up. And even if he did dare to climb out the window, head over to his producer's apartment, strangle him and then return, it would have taken at least two hours on a return journey. How could he have been answering the knocks on the door in the gaps between?"

The lanky spinner bounded in and delivered the ball. It landed in front of the defensive prod of the batter and spun sharply past him.

"Niii-iiiice, Garry," bellowed the wicket-keeper, as the ball bounced off his clumsy gloves to the short leg fielder, who picked it up and tossed it back to the bowler.

The detective recorded the dot ball and turned back to Vickers.

"Maybe Huber set up a live audio stream and listened in via his phone for the knocks at the door and then replied to the staff via that same connection," the detective suggested.

"Impossible," said Vickers. "The Dead Zone is proudly internet-free. It contains no wi-fi and no mobile phone connectivity. It's marketed as an 'online detoxification centre'. That's why Huber records there - to avoid distra—."

The detective suddenly joined the roar of the Gabbatoir crowd and stood to applaud as the next ball was squeezed between bat and pad, rebounding straight into the hands of the diving short leg.

"Nice, Garry," he shouted, continuing to applaud, only stopping when the batter called for a review. He sat back down. "You were saying?" he said to Vickers.

"I was talking about avoiding distraction," said Vickers.

"Ah," said the detective. "So if there's no internet connectivity, Huber can't possibly have been talking to the staff remotely. And he can't have prerecorded his responses, because he couldn't have known when they'd knock on the door."

"Exactly," said Vickers.

"Maybe, and bear with me here," said the detective. "Maybe Huber didn't do it. Do you have a motive?"

"Not really," admitted Vickers. "We're assuming it's probably something to do with not wanting to share those lucrative Squarespace advertising dollars."

"And you haven't considered the possibility of any of the podcast hosts currently above him on the charts, who might consider Huber and his producer a threat to *their* advertising cashflow?"

"Of course we have," said Vickers, clearly lying.

"Because I'm hearing you talk about a computer that could easily have been fried by a cattle prod. Or a murder that could have been committed by people so obsessed by the topic that they break down a genuine modern pop music classic as an excuse to talk about it. Or Billy Moore, widely acknowledged as a former rugby league player and, hence, capable of almost any atrocity." The detective tried to angle his head so he could see past the smudges that covered his glasses to the third umpire review taking place on the big screen. Unsuccessful, he turned back to Vickers. "Any of those three could easily be considered viable suspects. So why focus on Huber, who seems to have an airtight alibi?"

Vickers looked warily from side to side, but nobody else was paying attention to him. They were all focused on the review, and the disappointing absence of any mark on Snicko.

"It's for the publicity mostly," admitted Vickers. "This kind of case, featuring a murder by an up-and-coming celebrity podcaster, could easily be turned into an eight-part Netflix streaming series. Between the two of us, that's something the Queensland Police Force are *very* interested in. We're thinking of calling it 'Jail Bird!'"

He pulled from a folder a promotional poster for the TV series that the QPF Marketing Division had mocked up. He displayed it proudly to the detective, who paid it no heed.

Instead, he grimaced as the decision was officially overturned by the third umpire. The onfield umpire crossed his arms in front of his legs in a half-hearted Charleston of negation, and finally, sadly, the detective turned back to Vickers.

He took the poster, looked at it for a moment, then handed it back.

"And you just need me to prove that Huber's actually guilty, despite the airtight alibi?" he said.

"Ideally."

"Well, you're in luck."

The detective has solved the mystery of how Huber could have been murdering his producer while simultaneously being in his hotel room across town. Can you*??*

DESPITE VICKERS' PLEAS, THE DETECTIVE OFFERED NO FURTHER information until the end of the over.

"The key to the mystery," said the detective, as the bowler took back his cap and placed it on his sweating, bald head. "Is what we just saw out there."

Vickers stared out to the middle, unsure what the detective was getting at.

"Every single fielder, and at least one umpire, was certain they'd heard that edge hit the bat. And yet it hadn't. The noise they'd heard was the bat hitting the boot." He smiled. "Similarly, the staff at The Dead Zone were convinced they'd heard Huber respond to their door knocks. And yet they hadn't."

"So what *did* they hear then?" asked Vickers.

The detective ignored the question. "If he wasn't in his hotel room that entire evening, we know he had plenty of time to carefully climb out the window, scale down to ground level, murder his producer and return to the room, where he could retrieve and eat his dinner."

The detective continued. "We also know Huber went to the same room in the same hotel to record multiple episodes of the podcast. He always turned the air-conditioning off and opened the window instead. Why? Well, it wasn't to avoid podcast noise. The consistent background hum of an air-conditioner is trivial to remove digitally."

"Then why?" asked Vickers

The detective smiled. "Because he was training one of his birds to fly into the room. A talking bird - maybe a parakeet or a cockatoo or a parrot. It doesn't matter what kind. It just needed to be a bird trained to respond to knocks at the door with one specific phrase: 'I'm still podcasting'. *That's* how an ornithologist sets up an airtight alibi."

Vickers nodded slowly. "You've cracked it, detective!" he said. "How can we possibly thank you?"

"In lieu of the usual fee, I simply want a 'Consulting Producer' credit on 'Jail Bird!' and 0.5% of the profits."

"Deal!" said Vickers, reaching out his hand.

"*Gross* profits," said the detective.

Vickers gulped. "Okay," he eventually said. "You've earned it."

Ha ha ha! He sure has! Stay tuned for further baffling mysteries that can only be solved by the sleuth of slower balls, the gumshoe of googlies, the investigator of inside edges: the Tragic Detective.

LOCK-DON

PILOT EPISODE (SEASON 1, EPISODE 1)

A *zany sitcom teleplay originally published in* The Pinch Hitter, *a digital publication launched in 2020 during the opening overs of the pandemic. I pitched this idea to the editor with an email header that correctly read* 'The stupidest pitch you'll receive'.

'The One Where The Guys Argue About Netflix'

FADE IN:

INT. LIVING ROOM - NIGHT

TONY LOCK, left-arm orthodox spinner for England, late 20s, doomed to be forever overshadowed by Jim Laker but doesn't know it, reclines on the couch in front of the television set.

LOCK
(yelling)
Come on, Donald. It's starting.

A head pokes into the room from the hallway. The head belongs to THE DON, Australian cricketer, mid-20s, the greatest batter in the history of Test cricket and definitely knows it.

THE DON pauses a beat as he waits for the applause and whooping from the studio audience to die down.

THE DON
What do you mean, 'it's starting'? It's Netflix. It starts whenever we want it to.

LOCK
Yes. And I want it to start right, bloody, now!

THE DON hurries into the room and sits precisely on the couch. He is wearing AN IMMACULATE PAIR OF PYJAMAS, with 'DGB' embroidered on the shirt pocket.

THE DON
What are we watching?

LOCK

That documentary everybody's raving about. It's called 'Tiger King'.

THE DON

(with head in hands, despite medical advice against such face-touching)

Oh no. Not another Bill O'Reilly leg spin masterclass.

The studio audience explodes with laughter, as we...

CUT TO:

OPENING CREDITS

A jaunty tune - The LOCK-DON THEME SONG - plays over a montage of classic scenes from the show: LOCK demonstrating his bowling technique. THE DON washing his hands. LOCK overturning a backgammon set while THE DON shrugs and smiles at the camera. Etcetera.

LOCK-DON THEME SONG LYRICS

"When Laker took 19, Lock was there to take one.

When Australia lacked runs, they called on The Don.

Now they're shut in together

Wielding willow and leather

An Aussie and Pom, here in LOCK-DON!"

ANNOUNCER (V.O.)

LOCK-DON is filmed before a simulated studio audience.

CUT TO:

INT. LIVING ROOM - NIGHT

As the first episode of 'Tiger King' ends, LOCK presses pause to prevent the next from automatically starting.

LOCK

It's like my father always said - a big cat monarchy simply doesn't work. You need to have either human beings or a representative democracy.

THE DON

I don't want to argue about politics again, Tony. Let's just watch the next episode.

LOCK

(shaking his head)

I don't want to watch any more TV tonight.

THE DON

Why not? It's not like we have anything better to do. After all, as you know, we're locked in quarantine for the foreseeable future because of the chronavirus that's swept across the timestream bringing together random cricketers from all different eras.

LOCK

That's right, and that seamless exposition reminds me: Have you heard from Willis & Grace recently?

THE DON

I FaceTimed™ with WG today. He's busy but hopeful that we can keep flattening the curve. 'Remaining isolated is the heavy roller,' he said.

(clapping his hands together)

So let's do it. Let's binge the rest of this show tonight.

LOCK

(irritated)

There you go again, Donald. It's always about quantity with you, isn't it? Watch all the episodes, break all the batting records, panic-buy all the toilet paper--

THE DON

You know I'm susceptible to getting the runs.

LOCK

(ignoring him)

But sometimes it's not about quantity. Sometimes it's about quality. Oh sure, Laker can take nineteen wickets in a Test and ten in an innings like a big show-off. But who was going to dismiss opener Jim Burke? Hmmm?

THE DON

Laker?

LOCK

(suddenly furious)

Only in the second innings! And only because I was there to take the catch off his bowling. Who got Burke in the first dig?

THE DON nods in tired acquiescence. He has heard this story dozens of times already.

LOCK (CONT'D)
(pointing to himself with two thumbs)
That's right. It was this guy. But does anybody ever talk about it?

DON
(staring straight down the camera and muttering)
I know *somebody* who talks about it.

The simulated studio audience laughs uproariously.

CUT TO:

INT. BEDROOM - NIGHT

LOCK and THE DON are getting ready for bed. LOCK is brushing his teeth. THE DON is bouncing a golf ball in the air using only a cricket stump.

THE DON
(counting the taps)
96... 97... 98... 99...

The final tap is almost as perfect as the rest but not quite. THE DON catches the golf ball and puts it in his pocket.

THE DON (CONT'D)
99.94... and done.

LOCK
(emerging from bathroom)
I'm sorry I lost my temper earlier. I guess I'm just going a bit stir crazy.

THE DON

That's okay. There were two of us out there. One of us wanted to watch more Netflix. The other did not.

LOCK

You're a good friend, Donald. In fact, you're my best friend.

The simulated studio audience goes 'awwww' and applauds.

THE DON

And you, Tony, you're... you're... you're a fine left-arm orthodox spinner.

As the simulated studio audience guffaws at THE DON's hilarious inability to verbalise any kind of human emotion, LOCK goes in for a hug, then catches himself. The pair bump elbows instead. They climb into their bunk beds and LOCK uses a clapper to turn off the light.

END CREDITS ROLL

LOCK

(in sudden understanding)

Ohhhhh... 'susceptible to getting the runs'. I get it now.

CLUMSY LEG BEFORE WICKET

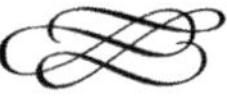

AN IDEA FOR FIXING CRICKET MATCHES

The sport of cricket is correctly acknowledged as the greatest sport of them all. But just because it's better than every other sport doesn't mean it can't be improved further.

Throughout this book I'll offer ideas for fixing cricket matches - proposals for changes to the Laws of the game (or tactical approaches to those Laws) that would add to the sport a fresh tactical, athletic or comedic dimension.

PROBLEM WITH CURRENT LAW

The current leg before wicket Laws have no aesthetic component to them. It is simply an umpire's opinion (augmented by ball-tracking technology where appropriate) on whether the ball will go on to hit the stumps, subject to the usual leg before wicket caveats.

PROPOSED SOLUTION

Margins of error for LBWs should be adjusted in proportion to how clumsy the batter has been made to look.

IMPLEMENTATION

If a bowler appeals for LBW, both umpires will immediately hold up a numbered card between 1 and 5. As with Olympic diving or gymnastics, those cards shall be a subjective measure of the aesthetic clumsiness of the batter in negotiating the delivery. The higher the number, the more awkward the batter has been made to look. (Note: This is the reverse of those subjectively scored Olympic sports - a variation that will help maintain the supremacy of cricket as a sport.)

The following Aesthetic Clumsiness Score (ACS) guidelines should be applied:

1. Batter plays a textbook defensive stroke that just happens to miss the ball
2. Batter is deemed to have initially misjudged the line or length of the ball but mostly recovers their composure by the time the ball reaches them
3. Batter seems befuddled by the bowler's skill and plays a panicky or belated shot at the delivery
4. Batter is *completely* deceived by movement in the air or off the pitch and is utterly wrong-footed and made to look like an inept child
5. Batter is knocked off their feet by an inswinging yorker like a total fucken idiot

The bowler's end umpire will then make their LBW decision as usual. However, in any aspects of the decision where there is an element of judgement to be made (did the ball pitch outside leg, was the batter struck in line with the stumps and, most importantly, would the ball have gone on to hit the stumps), the umpire shall adjust their opinion in accordance with the combined total of the umpires' Aesthetic Clumsiness Scores.

Again, as a guideline:

- An ACS of 1-3: the batter should be given the benefit of the doubt with no mental adjustment to any LBW judgements
- An ACS of 4-6: start to give the bowlers an advantage in any judgement adjustment (eg "Did that pitch outside leg? Well, maybe just a little bit. Who cares?")
- An ACS of 7-9: the bowlers should be given all possible leeway for the decision (eg "Don't care where it pitched or whether it struck in line - if it's in the general vicinity of the stumps, I'm giving it.")
- An ACS of 10: Out. Who cares about actual Laws at this stage? The batter looks like a fool. Get them outta here.

PROS

- A bowler is rewarded for their ability to make a batter look foolish, arguably a more impressive feat than merely dismissing them
- Gets the square leg umpire involved in leg before wicket dismissals
- Adds a new statistic by which batters and bowlers can be measured
- Also, a new acronym - ACS (Note, in line with other cricketing terminology vagueness such as 'innings', the ACS will be used to refer both to 1) either one of the

umpire's scores or 2) the combined total of the scores. Cricket fans will be forced to infer which of the two meanings is intended based on context.) Ideally, ACS will also be usually spoken of as an 'ACS score' (despite 'score' being part of the acronym) to infuriate pedants

CONS

- There will be initial difficulties in coding these changes into the ball-tracking algorithms used for DRS. Not so much for the alteration to the margins of error. That should be a simple mapping from the umpires' ACS score to a ball-tracking and projection adjustment factor. But if we wish to ultimately also refer the onfield ACS to a computerised check, that will require more sophisticated analysis. However, some kind of machine learning study of video footage of the batter's awkwardness and the ensuing scores should be well within the capabilities of modern computers, given enough example data. Once this technology is settled, the batter would have to specify which aspect of the decision they wish to review - the umpires' ACS scores *or* the ensuing decision based on those scores. (A particularly bold batter could burn two reviews and check both)
- Holding up the score cards will take a few seconds more time on each LBW appeal, as the bowler's end umpire both takes into consideration the square leg umpire's input, and adds a suitably dramatic pause before revealing their decision based on the ACS

FURTHER NOTES

It is acknowledged that many umpires are already influenced to some extent by how foolish the batter has been made to appear. This is a correct instinct and the proposed change to this Law seeks merely to codify that factor.

FORGING A NEW SPIRIT

A version of this piece was originally published over on Cricket365.com during the heady days of the 2019 World Cup. Luckily, I've stripped the piece of as many references to that tournament as possible. Let us not speak of it again.

Cricket is always evolving, always exploring new ground, always changing. Like some kind of mutant bulldozer-based Transformer.

But as cliched as it is to compare this magnificent sport to Rampage™ the Constructicon™ from *Transformers: Revenge of the Fallen,* that doesn't make the point any less true. Quite the reverse, in fact.

Batters have a greater array of preposterous strokes at their disposal, and wield them fearlessly via their notorious bigger bats. Bowlers, in turn, have developed such a variety of slower balls that it leaves one wondering if some deliveries will ever reach the other end. And, of course, fielders are nowadays always dancing fleet-footedly around the boundary's edge, juggling the ball with synchronised precision, like the synchronised boundary-dancing jugglers we've always wanted them to be.

And yet, one area of the game hasn't moved on.

I refer, of course, to the Spirit of Cricket, which still hovers around grounds, slurringly urging players to walk and tut-tutting mankads like the inebriated spectre of a 19th century Jane Austen matriarch that it self-evidently is.

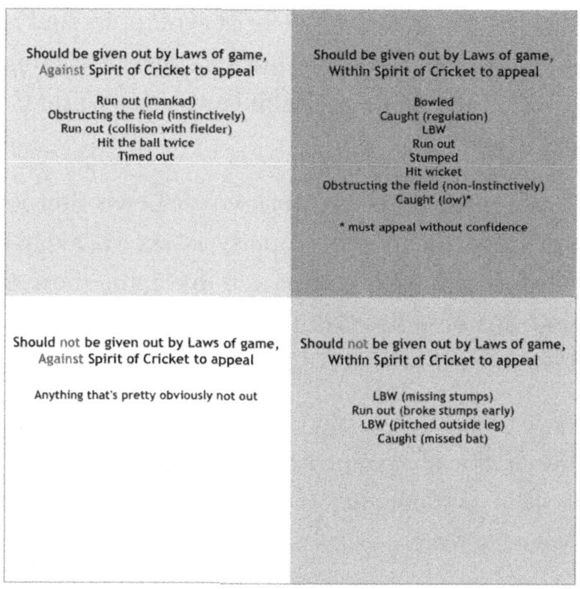

Should be given out by Laws of game, Against Spirit of Cricket to appeal	Should be given out by Laws of game, Within Spirit of Cricket to appeal
Run out (mankad) Obstructing the field (instinctively) Run out (collision with fielder) Hit the ball twice Timed out	Bowled Caught (regulation) LBW Run out Stumped Hit wicket Obstructing the field (non-instinctively) Caught (low)* * must appeal without confidence
Should not be given out by Laws of game, Against Spirit of Cricket to appeal	**Should not be given out by Laws of game, Within Spirit of Cricket to appeal**
Anything that's pretty obviously not out	LBW (missing stumps) Run out (broke stumps early) LBW (pitched outside leg) Caught (missed bat)

Current Spirit of Cricket guidelines - far too complicated

And so, putting aside the genuine possibility that suggesting the Spirit of Cricket needs updating is, in itself, a violation of the Spirit of Cricket, what I'd like to do here is propose an update to the Spirit of Cricket.

After all, it's one thing to suggest that batters should walk when they feather one through to the keeper. But that's hardly necessary these days, is it? Not when, in the immortal words of third umpire Rod Tucker, we have, 'whaddayacallit, UltraEdge' to sort such things out. Any batter not walking in the modern game is only delaying the rock'n'rolling inevitable.

No, a form of walking more fitting with the 21st century lifestyle would surely be for a batter to notice that a ball has hit the stump, failed to dislodge those pigheaded zing bails, and yet, with a nod of acceptance to the bowler, leave the batting crease anyway.

It's the kind of thing Adam Gilchrist would do, and therefore it's the kind of thing any big-hitting, wicket-keeping, game-changing batter should do. Rishabh Pant, your World Cup semi-final moment awaits.

Similarly, while we have the Duckworth Lewis Stern methodology to guide us on how to properly assess the likely outcome of a cricket match that's impacted by rain, these spineless professors insist on only making a call once a certain minimum number of overs are bowled.

But as we've seen often in big tournaments, that minimum over benchmark is not always possible to achieve. So until we can convince these mathematical yellow-bellies to probabilistically step up, we need to rely on cricket captains.

If a match between Bangladesh and England were to be washed out in a World Cup, for example, then the Bangladesh skipper - who we shall assume, for ease of marketing, is Shakib Al Hasan - needs to look at the official ICC ODI rankings, unbiasedly assess the form of both teams and magnanimously offer Jos Buttler - or whoever's taking his place while he's having an ECB-mandated rest or promoting The Hundred - the point Bangladesh would otherwise have unjustly earned from the inclement weather. It's the right thing to do in a tournament of such importance. Why the Spirit of Cricket doesn't already cover this is beyond me.

There are other ways of modernising the Spirit of Cricket too.

A team runs out of reviews because a disappointed batter puts fist to forearm without thinking the moment through? Give them that review back.

A mysteriously not-quite-retired-yet Chris Gayle wants to run a single? Churlish to even attempt a run out.

The television coverage awards your team a phase you don't feel you fully won? Offer to share it with your opponents.

The options are endless.

Furthermore, with all these upgrades to The Spirt of Cricket, an entire rebranding of the concept needs to be considered. And, like all cricket rebrandings, it should appeal to as wide a market as possible (ie, India).

May I humbly suggest this new Spirit of Cricket be reimagined as the Kohli Konscience. This opens up a marketing opportunity that I'm sure the ICC will not hesitate to exploit. After all, how much would you pay to have a tiny Virat Kohli doll that could sit on your shoulder and whisper ethical advice to you? Answer: the entire quantity of your local currency that's currently in your possession.

Pinocchio had Jiminy Cricket to teach him right from wrong. And yet, despite the surname, Jiminy was never once ranked the best batter in the world. Not in any of the three major formats. This is not a problem with the Kohli Konscience, and the ICC therefore need not limit their moral guidance to demonic marionettes brought to unholy life with dark Disney magic.

The Kohli Konscience can instead teach *all* of us to be virtuous (*virat*uous?), whether we be international cricketer, weak-minded administrator or awestruck spectator.

And, as such, the Spirit of Cricket is no longer needed to guide us. We can, at long last, move on and leave it behind us. Rest easy, you judgemental old phantom.

THE PAT CUMMINS GUIDE TO HANDSOMELY DOING CRYPTIC CROSSWORDS

While waiting for my opportunity to arrive at the batting crease to sort out the mess that the top order has invariably made of the innings, I'll often fill in time by handsomely doing a cryptic crossword.

A cryptic crossword is like an ordinary crossword that any child or wicketkeeper might attempt, but with an added element of wordplay that makes it vastly more compelling.

In this short guide to cryptic crosswords, I'll explain the basics of attractively solving these seemingly incomprehensible clues. That way, after you've humiliated some of the top ranked batters in the world with late seam and swing movement that sees them groping ineffectively at your every delivery before inevitably losing their wicket to one that jags back in and clips the top of off stump, you can sit back in the dressing room and relax, Adonis-like, with a good old-fashioned cryptic crossword.

THE BASICS

Virtually all cryptic clues can be divided into two basic parts:

1. A normal definition, similar to what you'd see in a boring crossword
2. Some sort of wordplay that also gives the same answer

The trick is that there's no way of knowing which part of the clue is which. That's why almost all cryptic crossword clues look like rampant gibberish to the untrained eye. Reading the entire sentence as a clue will almost never offer you any insight into the correct answer and it's why I refuse to allow any of the all-rounders (*especially* Marcus) to ever offer their thoughts.

Instead, you must gorgeously tease out which part of the clue is the normal definition and which is the wordplay. This is the easy-on-the-eyes fun of doing a cryptic crossword.

THE WORDPLAY

There are many types of wordplay involved in a cryptic crossword. Here are some examples:

ANAGRAMS

Anagrams are a very common form of wordplay, and often the easiest place to get started while looking like a prince among men. Look for *anagram indicators* - words that suggest that something is scrambled or rearranged or broken or weird or off or otherwise messed up. Also, take a smart, sophisticated, clean-cut look for words that seem an awkward fit into the clue. That often suggests they might be part of an anagram.

Pat Cummins Cryptic Tip: Before trying to telegenically rearrange the letters in a suspected anagram, check if the number of letters matches the number of letters in the answer. If they don't, you're on the wrong track.

Example

Abnormal TV airheads turn to number five (6,4)

Here, the anagram indicator is the word 'abnormal' and the letters that form the anagram come from 'TV' and 'airheads'. Rearranging those letters while sporting a dazzling smile that brings life to all who witness it soon gives 'TRAVIS HEAD', Australia's thrilling number five batter.

Note: the phrase 'turn to' is a joining phrase that joins the two clues together.

HIDDEN WORDS

Sometimes the answer is right before your piercing blue eyes, but hidden inside a phrase. If the wordplay is this type of clue, then there will usually be a hidden word indicator such as 'in', 'among', 'within', etc.

Example

Goat batted brilliantly, once in (4)

Here, the answer is obviously 'LYON', who is not only Australia's greatest ever off-spinner, but whose name also appears *in* 'brilliantLY ONce'.

Pat Cummins Cryptic Tip: In cryptic crossword clues, punctuation is generally meaningless, much like the social media missives of some of our more fidgety batters. Ignore punctuation.

REVERSALS

No, I'm not talking about Glenn Maxwell's love of a switch hit! Ha ha ha! I'm talking instead about clues that only make sense when you reverse them, all the time exhibiting the compelling self-confidence of a physically perfect specimen. As with the other kinds of clues, there will be an indicator phrase that tips you off that something is backwards - 'going back', 'reflected', 'turned over', etc.

Example

Dazzling debutant gave a tabloid newspaper back (4)

'Tabloid newspaper' = 'RAG'. Putting it *back* gives 'GAR' which, when joined with the 'a' (as in '*a* tabloid newspaper') returns the answer of 'AGAR', Australia's beloved debutant in the 2013 Ashes, who scored a thrilling 98 as a teenager batting at eleven. Great stuff.

Note: This clue also shows how you can build up answers from partial pieces of wordplay while being radiantly exquisite. The 'a' here is unchanged but gets the wordplay on 'rag' appended to it to give the correct answer.

ACROSTICS

"What's an acrostic?", those of you who are ill-educated young all-rounders fast-tracked into the side might be asking. An acrostic is simply a word made up of the first letters of other words. As always, you'll be given a hint about what's up, this time with acrostic indicators such as 'firstly' or 'initially' or 'at first'.

Example

Maybe all runscorers need unusual shots to begin with, suggests top batter (6)

The 'to begin with' indicator virtually implores you to inspect the first letter of the first six words of this clue with the dazzling majesty of a living angel. Which gives the answer 'MARNUS', Australia's magnificent number three and (at the time of writing) the top-ranked Test batter in the world.

Note: The 'suggests' is another joining word. The cryptic clue *suggests* the answer to the normal clue.

Pat Cummins Cryptic Tip: Of course, if you see indicators such as 'lastly' or 'ultimately' or 'at the end', you'd start looking at the letters at the ends of words too. The wordplay is limited only by the puzzle creator's imagination.

HOMOPHONES

Time to get homophonic! (But seriously, check the spelling there. The Australian cricket community is wholly inclusive and supportive of the entire LGBTQIA+ community.) A homophone is a word that sounds the same as another word. In a cryptic crossword clue, you'd be given an indicator that this is what's going on via terms such as 'spoken' or 'I hear', and that would be where you'd begin solving it in a breathtaking manner that exhibits pure aesthetic sublimeness.

Example

Swing bowler in the channel, I hear (6)

A channel is a 'chute', which (I hear) sounds like 'SCHUTT', the Australian women's team's thrilling swing bowler, who can make the ball move like nobody's business and often gets early wickets to set Meg Lanning's all-conquering side on the path to yet another dominant victory.

DOUBLE DEFINITION

Sometimes there's no real wordplay in the clue at all and, in fact, it's secretly just two normal clues back to back. This is a double bluff cryptic clue where you're *looking* for wordplay and instead everything is quite literal. Tricky!

Example

Opener will adopt the spirit of cricket before running the non-striker out (6)

The answer here, of course, is 'WARNER', which is both Australia's pugnacious opening batter and also somebody who *warns* a non-striker before mankading them.

Remember: a cryptic crossword clue is a piece of fun designed for entertainment and mental exercise while being staggeringly good-looking. It is not the same as real life, where it is, in fact, perfectly acceptable to mankad the living criminy out of any fool batter backing up too far without offering any warnings whatsoever.

OTHERS

There are many other different types of wordplay employed by cryptic crossword setters. But this should be enough to get you started. Good luck handsomely solving your cryptic crosswords.

Final Pat Cummins Cryptic Tip: And remember, not *every* answer to a cryptic crossword clue is a great Australian cricketer. More than 80% are other kinds of words completely.

Also available in the Pat Cummins Handsome Guide series, proudly published by Cricket Australia: *The Pat Cummins Guide To Handsomely Bowling Fast, The Pat Cummins Guide To Handsomely Captaining A Cricket Team* and *The Pat Cummins Guide To Handsomely Installing Rooftop Solar Panels*

CRYPTIC CROSSWORD 1

21ST CENTURY ASHES

Across

1 Fast bowler is manic stump scatterer (3,7)

5 Looked towards fine leg (7)

7 Heroic adventurousness inspires glee. Eyes on the opening pairs (10)

8 Cameron was happily leading a series thrashing (9)

13 He's smashed up at ribs! Ow! (8)

14 An innings, okay? (3)

15 He bowls wide (5)

16 I invent keeper's ill-nature (5,9)

21 &3D Radicals might strangely claim he's an all-rounder? (4,9)

22 Contains cherries? No. (4)

23 A terrible way to start the Ashes? (5)

24 An England captain who is a half-Australian blend seems extreme (7)

26 A fan of Haddin? (7)

30 The captain is planning to lose an opener (7)

31 Remove this shot (3)

32 Joan has a devastating yorker (5)

34 In the MCG, rather enjoying the bowling (7)

36 Leader put under pressure (3)

37 Dyson to the bowling crease? Or somebody else. (7)

38 A valid observation about a fielder (5)

Down

1 He will not ping wildly. He'll hit the stumps (7)

2 Bad grammar shouldn't limit a cricketer (5)

3 See 21A

4 Spare an enigmatic spinner (7)

6 Do some A/B testing on this Law (3)

9 Better than 11D, comparatively speaking? (6)

10 Frequently injured in an Ashes town (5,6)

11 Sounds like the pitch is sufficiently crumbling for the spinner (5)

12 The foundation of England's batting (4)

14 Name the most bizarre thing you'll see from Steve Smith in the middle (8)

16 He saw Cork zip it all around (10)

17 One of cricket's greatest fans (6)

18 2D? No, I improbably started as badly as 23A (8)

19 I hear he's a Transylvanian version of 11D (7)

20 The reason for more bowling. Or less. (2,4)

25 A captain with awfully inept aim (3,5)

27 The bowler took the head off a person and got on top (8)

28 36A's method (2)

29 Unsure why he's out (7)

33 Fix the captain (4)

35 Heavy scoring (3)

EXCERPT FROM ‘WISDEN FOR SMURFS’

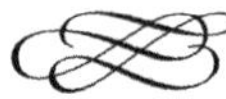

In a fit of marketing madness, Wisden once released a special blue edition of their cricketing bible targeted at Smurfs. It was not a success.

Match Report - Smurferset v Leicestersmurf

On a smurfy day in Smurferset, Leicestersmurf smurfed the toss and elected to smurf. Seam Bowler Smurf opened the bowling for Smurferset and smurfed the conditions smurfingly. At lunch, Leicestersmurf were 51/6 but a smurfing century from First Drop Smurf saw them recover to 204 all smurfed.

In response, Smurferset made 365, with Big Hitting Lower Order Smurf making a career smurfiest score of 83 not smurfed. Needing 161 just to make Smurferset smurf again, the visiting smurfs succumbed to smurfy bowling from Wily Off-Spinning Smurf to be dismurfed for 180. Smurferset's openers Opener Smurf and Matt Renshaw then smurfortlessly smurfed off the twenty runs required for a smurfy victory.

Smurf of the match: Best Player Smurf

NET BACK - A FAB FOUR DOCUMENTARY

When four young up-and-coming batters talked their way into Martin Crowe's offices, the veteran cricket producer sensed something special in them and immediately signed them to his label. Martin christened the quartet The Fab Four and sat back to watch as the talented tyros went on to change pop cricket forever.

FADE IN:

INT. GABBA ROAD STUDIOS, DAY

In between cricket gear scattered all around the studio sit THE FAB FOUR - VIRAT KOHLI, STEVE SMITH, KANE WILLIAMSON and JOE ROOT - as they plan and discuss their new venture together.

VIRAT KOHLI
(wearing round glasses and talking in a Liverpudlian accent)
Righto, lads. Time to make a new record. Do we have any ideas on what kind of record it should be?

JOE ROOT
(baby-facedly)
Most runs in a calendar year?

KANE WILLIAMSON
(quietly)
Most Spirit of Cricket Awards?

STEVE SMITH
(as if narrating 'Thomas the Tank Engine')
Best Test average?

VIRAT KOHLI
(wryly laughing)
Well, we're certainly the most divided we've ever been at this juncture in our long and storied history together. Thank goodness we've got a documentary crew filming every moment for posterity.

JOE ROOT
Is he going to be sitting in on this entire net session?

VIRAT KOHLI
Peter Jackson? Of course. How else is he going to document this?

VIRAT KOHLI gives a thumbs up to PETER JACKSON, who breaks off from discussing A RUINOUS SFX SCENE that inexplicably contains wargs and digital barrels and ANDY SERKIS, to return the gesture.

PETER JACKSON
Just ignore me. I'm a fly on the wall.

STEVE SMITH
(startled)
You're a what?!

JOE ROOT
No. Not Jackson. Him!

JOE ROOT points at RISHABH PANT, who is dressed entirely in black, his long hair parted down the middle and draping down to the floor. He SITS QUIETLY ON A CRICKET KIT in the background, writing haikus on the back of a ladybird using a quill and a magnifying glass.

VIRAT KOHLI
Rishabh? Oh sure. But don't worry. He won't disturb us.

STEVE SMITH
(screaming)
He'll break up the FAB FOUR!

JOE ROOT
(trying to restore focus)
Settle down, lads. Let's just focus on the work. Who has an idea for a single?

KANE WILLIAMSON
(quietly)
I'd like to nurdle one off my hip.

JOE ROOT
(ignoring him)
Anybody? Virat?

But VIRAT KOHLI is too busy joking around with RISHABH PANT to answer him. Instead, we zoom in on STEVE SMITH, who is pottering around with a bat. He starts jamming out SOME OF HIS FAVOURITE LEAVES.

JOE ROOT nods, picks up the rhythm and joins in. Soon the entire FAB FOUR is leaving with seasoned skill, each of them contributing to THE NON-PLAYING OF A CRICKET BALL in their own unique way, but blending together to create something that will yet again transform our understanding of THE POSSIBILITIES OF POP CRICKET.

The groove eventually comes to a natural end.

JOE ROOT
I like that one. What do you call it?

STEVE SMITH
Haven't got a name for it yet.

KANE WILLIAMSON
(quietly)
You should call it 'Leave It Be'.

JOE ROOT
(ignoring him again)
I'd call it 'Sgt Devereux's Goofy Off Stump Leave'

STEVE SMITH
(uncertain)
Yeah, maybe.

JOE ROOT
I really think it's a good name.
(clapping his hands together to change the subject)
Now. Let's talk about where we're going to perform these new pieces we've been working on.

STEVE SMITH
Is there a World Cup any time soon?

JOE ROOT
(consulting the ICC calendar)
There's a T20 World Cup in October. And, uh, January. Then an ODI World Cup in May. Then another T20 World Cup in July. Also, August. A World Test Championship in November. Then a Champion's Trophy in December. Along with another T20 World Cup.

VIRAT KOHLI
Doesn't seem special to perform at any of those, then, does it?

KANE WILLIAMSON
(quietly)
Maybe we could just perform on a rooftop here at Gabba Road.

JOE ROOT
(still ignoring him)
Okay, we'll come back later to the question of where we'll play. Let's instead now go through what we'll be playing. Steve has just come up with 'Sgt Devereux's Goofy Off Stump Leave'--

STEVE SMITH
(interrupting)
We may still find a different name for that.

JOE ROOT
(steamrollering on)
Sure. Maybe. And Virat's really keen on 'The One After 99'.

VIRAT KOHLI
I am really eager to return to playing that one as soon as possible.

JOE ROOT
(nodding)
Understood. Now I've come up with 'Net Back', 'Don't Put Me Down', and, like, half a dozen others. So I think between the three of us, we'll be able to put on a really good show.

KANE WILLIAMSON
(quietly)
Four.

JOE ROOT
Hmmm?

KANE WILLIAMSON
(quietly)
There's four of us.

JOE ROOT
(as if talking to a child)
Rishabh doesn't count, Kane, remember? He's just here to watch. Right, Virat?

VIRAT KOHLI looks up from chatting with RISHABH PANT. He clearly has no idea what JOE ROOT just said. He smiles, nods and returns to his MORE ENTHRALLING PANT CONVERSATION.

KANE WILLIAMSON

No, me.

JOE ROOT

(chuckling)

You've got something, Kane?

KANE WILLIAMSON

I do. I'm trying to capture the ineffable delight I feel in watching Sophie Devine bat. Something in the way she drives, she smacks it, like, through the covers.

JOE ROOT

(condescendingly)

You keep working real hard at that one, Kane.

KANE WILLIAMSON

(quietly)

I call it 'Here Come The Runs'.

VIRAT KOHLI

(looking up from his conversation with RISHABH PANT)

Hey, Joe. We should just play on the rooftop here at Gabba Road.

JOE ROOT

(excited)

Great idea!

STEVE SMITH

And what if I call my piece 'Leave It Be'?

JOE ROOT
(equally excited)
Fantastic!

KANE WILLIAMSON
(quietly)
Oh, for fuck's sake. That's it. I'm leaving the FAB FOUR.

KANE WILLIAMSON storms out of the Gabba Road studios.

STEVE SMITH
(screaming and pointing at RISHABH PANT)
I told you this would happen.

CUT TO:

EXT. GABBA ROAD STUDIOS, DAY

KANE WILLIAMSON is preparing to cross the road. There is no pedestrian crossing to iconically traverse, so he dutifully waits for the 'DON'T WALK' sign to change to 'WALK'.

But he is in Australia, so it never does.

THE SELECTION MEETING

A ruthless cull of an underperforming team eventually leads to a discussion about the future of the wicketkeeper.

"Now, what about the keeper?"

- *"I'm inclined to keep her."*

"I think there have been too many drops."

- *"Agreed. We've dropped too many. We need to keep her."*

"No, *she's* dropped too many. We need to drop her."

- *"It's tough to drop a keeper."*

"Tougher still to keep a dropper."

- *"Has she really dropped that many?"*

"She's dropped enough that there's no cause to keep her."

- *"But she's only dropped that many* because *she's the keeper."*

"Are you saying we should keep her because she's dropped so many?"

- *"I'm saying a keeper gets a lot of chances, which will lead to more drops."*

"Personally, I don't think she should have *any* more chances."

- *"Because she's had so many drops?"*

"Exactly. That's why she should be dropped."

- *"I think she should get one more chance before being dropped."*

"I'd hate to see another dropped chance."

- *"So you're saying* no *more chances."*

"Not if they're going to be dropped."

- *"Well, if she gets no more chances, there will be no more drops."*

"If you could guarantee no more drops, I'd be happy to give her another chance."

- *"I can't guarantee no more drops. It depends on the number of chances."*

"Oh, I think at most she only gets one more chance."

- *"If she only gets one more chance then it's unlikely there'd be* any *drops."*

"And that's why you're adamant we should keep her?"

- *"I just don't think it's time yet for goodbyes."*

"Well, there's no such thing as *good* byes. Not for a keeper."

- *"So you* wouldn't *say goodbye?"*

"Never."

- *"So does that mean you now want to keep her?"*

"Oh no. I still want to drop her." (Pause) "But there is a catch."

- *"A catch for the keeper?"*

"Yes."

- *"A catch to do with her dropping?"*

"Yes. Because I'd still like to keep her as a batter."

- *"But not as a keeper."*

"Exactly."

- *"But I don't think we can keep her as a batter. We can only bat her as a keeper."*

"Agreed. And that's the catch with dropping her."

- *"So because of this dropped catch, we have to keep her?"*

"Keep her as a keeper, yes."

- *(whistles in admiration) "That's some dropped catch."*

(with sincere apologies to Joseph Heller)

LEHMANN AND THE DEMON - A NETFLIX ORIGINAL SERIES

The first season of this paranormal reimagining of the reign of Australian cricket coach Darren Lehmann delves into the dark forces at play in the 2013 and 2013/14 Ashes series.

Supernatural - Witty - Cricket

EPISODE 1

Shortly after taking the reins of the Australian cricket team in 2013, new coach Darren 'Boof' Lehmann (Dean Norris) is visited by a supernatural creature - Fred 'The Demon' Spofforth (Henry Cavill). The unholy fiend demands the sacrifice of a goat (Nathan Lyon) in exchange for the promise of an Ashes victory. But Lehmann is not the only one accessing dark forces...

EPISODE 2

Undone by the malevolence of Stuart Broad (Owen Wilson), Lehmann is tempted again by The Demon, who offers to unleash even more powerful dark forces. The coach hesitates, but after a crushing defeat he agrees to the beast's demand for a sacrificial virgin (Ashton Agar). However, the deal comes with unforeseen repercussions, and the return of an unwelcome menace...

EPISODE 3

The return of David Warner (Jesse Plemons) to the side has Lehmann second-guessing the deals he's made with The Demon. In a series of flashbacks to the Walkabout bar, we learn exactly why Lehmann is so wary, before a stunning flash-forward hints at trouble in the future...

EPISODE 4

Another defeat sees a furious Lehmann confront The Demon, demanding the unholy imp keep his end of the assorted bargains they'd made. But when The Demon reveals that he never promised Lehmann *which* Ashes series he'd win, the desolate coach ponders his options...

EPISODE 5

With the Ashes lost, a distraught Lehmann reveals the extent of his supernatural dalliances to his first drop, seasoned ghost-hunter Shane Watson (Chris Hemsworth). Watson helps Lehmann lure The Demon into a dressing room pentagram, where the coach extorts several advantages from the hell-dwelling monster...

EPISODE 6

Three months later, we learn the first of Lehmann's renewed deals with The Demon. His demand that Mitchell Johnson

(Rami Malek) not only find form but also maintain it for an entire Ashes campaign begins promisingly. But there are hints that The Demon has his own schemes brewing...

EPISODE 7

The second of Lehmann's deals with The Demon is revealed, as Brad Haddin (Mickey Rourke) continues to wield chaos magic. The wicket-keeper's batting creates a probabilistic maelstrom that threatens the space-time continuum, but also allows Australia to take a 2-0 lead in the Ashes.

EPISODE 8

Each stride of Ryan Harris's (*Rhinocerotidae*) run-up to bowl the first ball of the second innings of the third Test brings us a flash back to further details of Lehmann's deal with The Demon. But the cost of a further year's worth of functioning knees for the big fast bowler may be far greater than Lehmann ever dared imagine...

(Note: Episode features the Grammy-award winning music video montage of Harris's eventual delivery backed by Nick Cave's cover of Walking on Sunshine*)*

EPISODE 9

With the Ashes regained, Lehmann attempts to summon The Demon again with an offer to renegotiate their dreadful blood pact. But despite the best efforts of Watson, the infernal fiend is nowhere to be found. Just as they begin to believe they're finally free of The Demon, a stunning post-credit scene reveals he's been with them all along...

EPISODE 10

In the season one finale, The Demon, now revealed to have escaped into the material world via the moustache of Mitchell Johnson, seeks new souls. As the Australians celebrate their Ashes whitewash, The Demon beckons a young Steve Smith (Jack Black) to the back of the dressing room where he makes him an offer...

THE ELEVEN XI

Selecting cricket elevens is a fine hobby. Selecting an eleven who have close ties to the number 11 is therefore finer still.

SELECTION GUIDELINES

- This is a Test XI
- Any player who still has an active career will not be considered, lest they ruin their 11-centric stats in the future
- Each position in the side must have a different cricket statistic with a value of 11 to justify selection
- An attempt should be made to diversify among as many nations as possible, but not if that weakens the eleven-ness of the team

THE ELEVEN XI

1. First up, we'll look at players who've played 11 Tests. One would imagine this will put a limit on the quality of the player. Nevertheless, in a brief career of 11 Tests, we have **Phil Jaques**, an Australian opener from 2005-2008 who scored 902 runs at 47.47, including three centuries. The standout candidate with an 11 Test career.
2. For our other opener, we'll do a bit of sneaky selecting and choose a player who made 11 stumpings in his career, former New Zealand captain **Brendon McCullum**. BMac mostly batted in the middle order in Tests, but he wasn't alien to opening. And, heck, it even looks like he has an 11 in his surname. He can open and keep.
3. At number three, we'll work with batters who've scored 11 centuries. Lots of choices here, including Nathan Astle, Hashan Tillakaratne and Ravi Shastri. But the late **Dean Jones**, with not only 11 centuries, but also 11 ducks and 11 not outs, has an irresistible claim to the spot.
4. At number four, it's time to consider players who've made 11 ducks. We could have used this in the opener slot and claimed Justin Langer, Gordon Greenidge or Graeme Smith. Or slotted in Kumar Sangakkara at first drop. But, again, it's an Australian with irresistible claims. This time, **Allan Border**, with 11 ducks, 11,174 runs, 11 Player of the Match awards and best bowling figures of 11/96.
5. We can get to our number five in the batting order by looking at players who've taken 11 wickets. Many fine candidates in here, but none finer than **Clyde Walcott**

who in his 44 matches, not only took 11 wickets but also completed 11 stumpings. Neat.

6. As we reach the bottom of the batting order, let's try players with 11 scores of fifty or more. Because if we do, we get to one magnificent name: **Douglas Jardine**. Not only 11 scores in excess of 50, but a career of 22 matches and 33 innings. Jardine will be our captain, fighting off a myriad of other contenders with the ruthless efficiency we've come to expect from him.
7. Let's find an all-rounder to bat at 7 by looking at who has been awarded Player of the Match on 11 occasions. In addition to the previously discussed Allan Border, we also have Shivnarine Chanderpaul, Shaun Pollock, Rahul Dravid and Glenn McGrath. But we especially also have **Imran Khan**, former Prime Minister of Pakistan, who scored 11 Player of the Match awards in 88 Tests, with a neatly divisible 8 Player of the Series awards.
8. Let's get serious about this bowling attack then. We'll choose another quick, one with best match figures that are an 11-fer. Zillions of players qualify for this, including Dale Steyn who once finished a Test with 11/60. As mentioned, we also have Allan Border. The best figures of Saeed Ajmal are very tempting at 11/111. Instead, with so many candidates, we're going to have to appeal to other factors, and **Geoff Lawson** not only has best figures of 11/134, but he also bowled 11,118 balls and took 11 five wicket hauls. That gets him a spot.
9. You know who also took 11 five wicket hauls? Andy Roberts and Bill O'Reilly. But also **Zaheer Khan**, who finished with 311 Test wickets and a batting average of 11.95. That'll do me. Sorry, Bill.
10. For our number ten slot, we'll look at players who finished their career with 11 catches. We could take

stars of Netflix's smash hit TV series *Lehmann and The Demon,* Darren Lehmann or Fred 'The Demon' Spofforth, here. But let's discard any semblance of Australian bias (apologies also to Bruce Edgar). No, instead we'll have West Indies great **Wes Hall**, thanks, easily the most experienced player to have taken a mere 11 catches, with 48 Tests.

11. Finally, for the number 11 in our eleven, we'll have a look at player contributions in the number 11 slot. Joel Garner is tempting, with his average of 11.00 while batting at 11, as is Darren Gough with his average of 11.11 for an even one hundred runs batting in the position. But the shameful oversight of Bill O'Reilly means the side still needs a spinner. And who better than the man who until recently made the most runs at number 11 of them all, **Muttiah Murilatharan**? Murali also averaged 11.67 overall and 11.32 at number 11. Could also bowl a bit.

I WOULD LIKE TO CLARIFY ONCE MORE THAT THE ASSERTION THAT THE UMPIRES WERE 'HOPELESSLY COMPROMISED CHEATS' WAS NOT MY OPINION BUT RATHER THAT OF MY VENTRILOQUIST'S DUMMY, CORPORAL BARMINGTON

In light of my recent fine from the match referee, I would like to stress, once again, the facts of the situation.

First, I ultimately accepted all the umpires' decisions - good *and* terrible - and told them so after the match. Sure, they made mistakes, some of them egregious ones that undoubtedly cost us the match. But we all make mistakes. And, as captain of the side, I understand that and would certainly never react disrespectfully to what several neutral observers have gone to great lengths to assure me were honest, human errors. In particular, I can't even imagine the circumstances under which I'd publicly imply that the officials who'd made those shocking calls had done so maliciously.

As we all now know, however, my ventriloquist's dummy, Corporal Barmington, has no such qualms. His claim that the umpires were 'hopelessly compromised cheats' was disappointing, even if it did accurately reflect what many of the fans that I bumped into after the match were saying. Did he go too far when he called them 'almost certainly corrupt' and 'the lowest form of humanity that has ever existed'? You'd have to say yes.

On reflection, it was perhaps a mistake to bring Corporal Barmington to the press conference, knowing how fiery and foul-mouthed he can get. Given his passionate reputation, maybe I should have been able to foresee that he would slam the third umpire as being 'too blind to acknowledge a mark on UltraEdge so spikey that it perhaps poked his idiot eyes out', accuse him of 'taking filthy money from foreign bookies' and demand that he be 'drawn and quartered by herds of water buffalo'.

Too far? Of course. But that's Corporal Barmington for you. He speaks his mind on cricketing matters and, to my way of thinking, that's how he's become so beloved in the greater cricketing community and why his appearances on podcasts can add hundred of thousands of new listeners to the download numbers of even the most tiresome of those self-indulgent ramblefests. Fans love his enthusiasm and unfiltered zeal for the game, even when he makes such outrageous claims that me and my team should have defecated in the officials' lunches because 'the umpires were so full of shit already that they wouldn't even notice'.

So, yes. Perhaps I should have left Corporal Barmington locked in the suitcase at the back of the dressing room. But I thought his presence might lighten the mood after a tense and undeserved defeat. How was I to know that the questions from the cricketing media would get him so fired up?

After all, while *I* did the right thing by pointing out that, from certain angles, you might make a plausible case that, perhaps, the ball had bounced before the catch was claimed, Corporal Barmington's opinions were more trenchant - calling the opposition 'the worst fucking swindlers in the history of the fucking sport - a disgrace to their muck-riddled nation, but also kind of what we expect from a country of degenerate lowlifes that have spent their entire cricketing history dragging everything down to their subterranean, inhuman level'. I'm pretty sure that was all just a bit of banter meant in good spirits even if, again, I personally think he's maybe going too far.

When the journalists asked him follow-up questions, you will notice that I very clearly took a long sip of water as Corporal Barmington exploded with fury, calling my opposing captain the 'most loathsome crook in the history of the sport' and 'the shittiest shitstain on the shit-riddled shithouse owned by the shittest of shit blokes'. Corporal Barmington's words, not mine. In fact, if you go back and study the footage of the press conference you will clearly hear me interjecting phrases such as 'no' and 'that's going too far, Corporal Barmington' as the venerated puppet got worked up into one of his infamous rants.

One of the other things I'd like to make clear is that Corporal Barmington's use of racial and ethnic slurs is definitely not on. Again, he's achieved his notoriety with his no-holds-barred opinions, and that's why he has such an enormous social media following. But his decision to resort to the crudest of stereotypes as he raged against the opposition and the umpires is definitely not one I endorse. In fact, you can clearly hear me exhaling in disappointment as Corporal Barmington makes his most outrageous slurs, something that, I think you'll agree, showcases once again that I don't agree with his controversial opinions.

I have been asked time and time again who, then, is the voice behind Corporal Barmington. And once more I'd like to make it clear that Corporal Barmington is his own puppet - a free-thinking cricket 'tragic' who doesn't go along with the woke thought police that so infest current day cricket cancel culture. He has his opinions and he'll share them and woe betide anybody who gets in his path. It's a bit of fun that even when it goes too far - like last month with some of his, frankly pretty disgraceful, insinuations about our magnificent women's cricket team - is the price of free speech.

So, again. No, we don't endorse any of the opinions of Corporal Barmington, but also yes, he will be present at the team announcement on Thursday, handing out caps to our debutants. Thank you for your time and, as Corporal Barmington would say, 'now fuck off back to your press box swill troughs, you subhuman pieces of detritus'.

SHANE WATSON - AUSTRALIA'S GREATEST EVER CAPTAIN

Was Shane Watson Australia's greatest ever captain? Of course he was. Let's go over the facts.

Who are the other major candidates in men's cricket? Sir Donald Bradman, captain of the Invincibles? Allan Border, the man who captained Australia in more Tests than anybody else? Steve Waugh, who won 72% of the Tests he captained?

Sure, these guys are perfectly competent leaders in their way, but their records are also all fundamentally limited. Not a single one of them ever captained Australia in a T20 international. Heck, Bradman didn't even captain Australia in an ODI. Do they even have even the faintest inkling of what it's like to be marshalling your field to try to stop a rampaging Virat Kohli, while simultaneously under the burden that your best remaining bowling options are Shaun Tait (3-0-58-0) and Joe Mennie (0-0-0-0)? They do not.

So, it only makes sense to consider those who have captained Australia in all three forms of the game. And that just leaves us with Ricky Ponting, Adam Gilchrist, Michael Clarke and Steve Smith as alternative greatest ever male captains.

Ponting first. And while Ponting has a good overall record on paper, we must never forget that the game isn't played on paper. It's scored on paper and played on grass, which I think we'll all agree is the best way to divvy up those two materials. Common sense, people.

But Ponting also lost the Ashes thrice. And that's careless captaincy at best. Watson is definitely well ahead of Ponting on this captaincy score, with his sole Test defeat as captain coming against India, who don't even compete for the Ashes. At least, not yet. Advantage Watson.

Over to Gilchrist, then, who, like Watson, was only ever considered as a stand-in captain. This is disappointing, because Gilchrist's captaincy record is, in fact, very good, most notably when he captained Australia to victory in a Test series against India in India. This victory was lauded as conquering the 'final frontier', despite the undeniable fact that Test cricket continued to be played after that point, tarnishing the claim somewhat. But it was still an outstanding achievement in leadership.

But Gilchrist, as most hardcore cricketing pundits will tell you, was also a wicket-keeper. And if there's one thing Australian selectors always knew in the fundamental core of their beings, right down beside the bit where you always select Shaun Marsh if the opportunity is there, it's that wicket-keepers shouldn't be captains.

The reasons for the discrimination against keepers were, for many decades, unclear, and it's always unsafe to delve too deeply into the mindsets of selectors. But I think the rationale was that keepers have too much on their mind to properly captain. Something to do with angles, I believe. You can't have a man captain a side when his head is full of trigonometry. That's a scientific fact. And the selectors were right. Look what happened to Tim Paine. Lesson learnt.

What about Michael Clarke, then? The captain with more funk than Rick James. Can Watson really be said to be a better captain than Superfreak Clarke?

And the answer is that of course he can. Let's put aside the Pontingesque fact that Clarke also lost the Ashes twice in England and compare the two solely on Clarke's *raison d'etre* of funkiness.

Shane Watson captained his sole Test against India, immediately after being suspended as part of HomeworkGate and flying home for the birth of his child. And in that Test he opened the batting and bowling with Glenn Maxwell. Yep. In one Test, Watson outfunked the entirety of Clarke's career. Case closed.

Steve Smith? Come on. As alluded to above, proper leaders get their suspensions out of their system *before* they take charge of a team. Smith got it completely the wrong way around. No contest.

It's pretty obvious then that Shane Watson is Australia's greatest ever cricket captain when compared to the other men who might stake a claim for that honour.

But it's not just men who play cricket, you sexist creeps. Belinda Clark, Karen Rolton, Jodie Fields, Alex Blackwell, Meg Lanning and Rachael Haynes have all captained Australia in all three forms of the game, winning Test series, World Cups and Commonwealth Games gold meals, hither and yon. Surely at least one of these must be on a par with Watson?

Well, maybe. But did any of them ever master the double fist pump roar of triumph when they took a wicket? Or burn the team's last review on a plumb LBW, then trudge off the ground sadder than Charlie Brown? Of course not. So Watto's got them all covered.

What about captains in other sports? John Eales? King Wally Lewis? Anne Sergeant? Johnny Warren? Lauren Jackson? None of those sports are cricket, so again, Watson has the advantage.

The facts are clear. Shane Watson is the greatest Australian captain of all time. Let's just make him the full-time captain of everything. The T20 team. The Test team. The starship Enterprise. Featherswords. Everything.

MOBILE SLOW OVER RATE EXTRA HALF HOURS

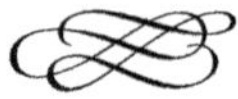

AN IDEA FOR FIXING CRICKET MATCHES

PROBLEM WITH CURRENT LAW

Slow over rates mean that almost every day of Test cricket has an additional half hour added to it, but, boringly, always in the final session.

PROPOSED SOLUTION

Test cricket should sprinkle the extra half hours throughout the Test, by allowing captains to delay lunch or tea or drinks by half an hour to try to exploit a tactical advantage or make the opposition hangry.

IMPLEMENTATION

Twice per Test (once while bowling, once while batting), a captain shall have the opportunity to delay a scheduled break (lunch, tea, drinks) by half an hour. As the umpire removes the bails or waves the drinks cart onto the field, either captain has ten (10) seconds to invoke the 'Keep Playing' gesture, by waving their arms across their face as if trying to hail down a passing car or get the attention of somebody on the other side of a music festival. That will be a signal for play to continue uninterrupted.

(If the captain is not on the field because their team is batting and they're not at the crease, they must ensure they attract the umpire's attention within the legislated time from either the dressing room or the boundary's edge.)

It is permissible for both captains to add an extra half hour of play, totalling to a full hour. This would be accomplished either by both making the Keep Playing gesture at the scheduled break, or one making it at the scheduled break, and then the other at the end of the extended period of play.

Of course, all time added to a session is purely additional. That is, it is *not* to be subtracted from the following session.

PROS

- The extra half hour added to a session is already an existing Test cricket notion, automatically applied under specific circumstances. This change should therefore integrate seamlessly into the structure of the match, satisfying traditionalists
- The extra half hour would make it more difficult for batters to merely set their sights on surviving the last few overs of a session, which in turn would encourage more attacking cricket
- Conversely, batters who are on top would not have to curtail their feasting on bowling ineptitude merely because a break was scheduled
- Fans could get as much as two hours' extra Test cricket in a day's play. Value for money!

CONS

- Technically, a Test match has five extra half hours in its current form, whereas this version provides only four. This could be compensated for by giving the captain who *loses* the toss an additional half hour extension to be implemented at their whim
- The option to make the players extra hungry or thirsty by extending the session could be undone by twelfthies running on secret drinks or snacks. This would need to be strictly policed by the umpires, much more strictly than they currently do. (Note: the umpires would also be denied a break, perhaps generating more errors in their decisions during the extended sessions. This factor would require teams to use their extended sessions and DRS reviews together in an optimised fashion)
- The sight of a captain at the boundary's edge or the balcony of the dressing room would potentially give away their intention to call for an extension to play. A savvy captain would, however, presumably use this to their advantage, either by bluffing their intention to extend or sneaking to the boundary's edge while wearing a disguise (eg a Ghostface costume)
- Catering staff would need to be more flexible with heating up the frozen lasagne

FURTHER NOTES

It is theoretically possible for the break to be extended by a full two hours, effectively adding an entire extra session. Here's an example of how:

- Captain A (batting) extends the session by half an hour

- At the end of the extended session, Captain 2 (bowling) further extends the session, and dismisses the opposition. They commence batting.
- Now, either Captain A or 2 could use their other extension to add yet another half hour to the session
- And finally, the other captain could wipe out the last of the extensions with one final half hour addition

Such a scenario, while rare, would be thrilling and would, ideally, be designated as a 'Quadruple Extension Four Hour Double Session'.

OH, WATTO NIGHT!

A TRAGIC DETECTIVE MYSTERY

I met the client at the bottom of the stadium. She radiated a furious intensity, like a project manager pretending to be human. She was in her early forties, but looked half a decade younger. Alternatively, she was in her early thirties, but looked half a decade older. It was impossible to know for sure.

"Do you like cricket?" I asked her.

"No."

"Good," I said. It always makes it easier if they don't get distracted by the match. I explained the etiquette to her as we headed up the stairs. How she shouldn't say anything to the detective until the end of the over. Also, what an 'over' was and how one might detect its end.

We reached our row and shuffled sideways past the empty seats to where the detective sat alone and immobile, like a head with its chicken cut off. Half a beer sat at his sprawled feet, and pie remnants flaked his T-shirt.

From the seat beside him, the detective picked up the tattered and malodorous straw hat he'd worn so fearlessly throughout the afternoon and evening sessions. He gestured to the client to sit down in its stead. She did so, remaining silent and staring at the Instagrammable sunset as she waited for some indication that the over had concluded. The detective's bespectacled gaze never left the cricket, and in particular the musclebound batter, as he survived a hostile over from the bowler, dotting out a maiden.

The detective finished updating his scorecard, applauded the batter's survival enthusiastically and drinks were taken. He turned to the client.

"Mrs Alvarado," he said, unwrapping a Kit Kat. "How can I help you?"

She wasted no time. The 'Drinks Break' option on the website is by far the cheapest, but it *does* come with the tightest time frame. We make it very clear when clients book that they need to ensure their story can be told in just a handful of minutes.

"My husband is a Social Media Influencer," she said, capitalising with disdain. "And I suspect he's having an affair with one of his followers."

She handed over her phone, with the screen logged into a Twitter account.

"Ah," said the detective, nodding and smiling knowingly. "@FrankieGoesToValliWood."

"You've heard of him?"

"No." The detective tapped around the phone, carelessly covering it with a veneer of melted chocolate.

"He's enormous in the Frankie Valli and the Four Seasons fan community," explained Mrs Alvarado. "Valli Girls hang on his every tweet."

"I see," said the detective. "And why do you think he's having an affair?"

"Detective, I don't need you to prove he's having an affair. I already know that in my heart."

"How so?" said the detective, belatedly wiping his hands on his shirt.

"Little things. His general air of distraction whenever we talk. His renewed interest in his deportment. His locked burner phone that I found in the cistern of our toilet. My husband's definitely having an affair, detective. I need *you* to tell me who he's having it with."

The detective nodded and gestured for her to go ahead. Out in the middle, one of the players fed sporting cliches to a flying robot.

"As you can see, my husband has over half a million followers, but only follows 43 people himself. I had our butler Gervais run an analysis on those followers. Here are the results."

She handed over a printout of a spreadsheet to the detective, who scanned down the list.

"The three Valli Girls he interacts with the most are @BigGirls-DontCritique, @LateDecember1993 and @CantTakeMyEyes-OffYou. Gervais was able to reverse-image search their avatars and find other social media profiles which he cross-matched to find their identities. That, and some judicious use of Google gave us the following information."

"Gervais is quite the hacker," said the detective, with a tone that I would have described as admiration, had I not known better.

"Twenty-first century butlering requires a diverse array of skills," smiled Mrs Alvarado, before going on to explain what she'd discovered on the three followers she'd highlighted.

"@BigGirlsDontCritique is Lacy Madison. She's physically the closest, living just a few suburbs away from us. There's little other reason to be suspicious of her. She and my husband chat regularly online - usually about Valli's early work - but it's generally innocuous stuff. Lots of talk about falsetto techniques and B-sides. However, her sheer proximity concerns me. She's certainly the most convenient fan for him to have an affair with."

The detective dropped the other half of his Kit Kat into his half-drunk beer. He retrieved it and finished it off, before downing the beer as well, for safety's sake. Mrs Alvarado continued.

"@LateDecember1993 is Sherry Nance. She has a blog where she writes thinly disguised erotic fiction about a prominent Social Media Influencer being stranded in a small country town where he's seduced by a brazen fan, while the song 'Sherry' plays in the background. She posts a new version of this same story twice a week on her blog."

"What's the name of the blog?" asked the detective, clearing his throat and pushing his glasses up his nose.

Mrs Alvarado told him and the detective tapped around her phone a little more, emitting what were presumably involuntary noises as he perused the blog.

"Could he have met her?" he asked.

"Yes," said Mrs Alvarado. "There are several ValliCons each year, and my husband is a much sought after speaker at them. And her home town is within driving distance of at least three of these conventions."

The detective barely seemed to be listening. He emitted a tiny 'wow' at the story he was reading. He placed Mrs Alvarado's phone down beside him for a moment and exhaled. Eventually, he gestured for her to continue.

"@CantTakeMyEyesOffYou is Victoria Starr. She's always the first one to like his tweets. She must be following him incredibly closely. They interact regularly, bantering back and forth. She's twenty years younger than him - which he doesn't seem bothered by, of course. She also looks exactly like me at the same age, except with less interest in dressing appropriately. Like @LateDecember1993, she lives interstate, but that does *not* seem to dissuade her from making lewd comments about how much she'd like to make him 'walk like a man'. Which, honestly, barely even makes sense in terms of innuendo."

The fluorescently-garbed drink carriers had by now left the ground. The batters began to strap their gloves back on.

"So, detective, can you tell me who my husband is cheating on me with?"

"I can," he said. "You've given my exactly enough information to solve this mystery."

The detective has solved the mystery of who @FrankieGoesToValliWood has been sleeping with. Can you*??*

Answer:* No, *you can't.* Stop *wasting your time puzzling over it and let the detective explain.

"One of the glorious things, Mrs Alvarado, about Test cricket is how the act of *not* playing a shot to a particular delivery can, in fact, be an example of excellent batting. We saw that in the over before drinks, when Watto deliberately refused to defend the moving ball under the twilight lights, in case it found his edge. It was outstanding cricket from the great man."

"Okay," said Mrs Alvarado, shrugging her shoulders at the apparent irrelevance of this information.

"Similarly, the key to solving this mystery is not the people with whom your husband interacts in public, but rather the ones with whom he *doesn't*. And so I point you to the bottom of your spreadsheet. To @FourSeasonsFourMillionReasons. He follows her. She follows him. They both interact regularly with other people. And yet they *never* interact with one another. That's suspicious to me."

The detective held up a hand to indicate that he had more to say, but he needed to watch this next delivery. The bowler charged in and strayed down leg side, allowing the man on strike to scurry a run. The non-striker lumbered through, with Panzer-like speed.

"In fact," continued the detective, as he recorded the leg bye in his scorecard. "There is only one tweet where the two of them are even tagged together. A reply from a mutual follower that tags them both and is simply an exclamation mark. And that reply was to a tweet which has since been deleted."

"I don't get it," said Mrs Alvarado.

"I'd posit to you," said the detective. "That the deleted tweet was a suggestive DM from one of them to the other which was posted accidentally and then hastily deleted, but not before this one follower saw it."

"But how do I prove any of this, detective?" asked the client. "Are you proposing I contact this exclamation mark follo—"

The detective again held up a hand to stop her. The bowler was running in once more. This time, the ball was straighter and it struck the batter on his enormous front pad. The fielders exploded into a loud appeal. The batter stared forlornly back at the umpire, eyes fixed on the adjudicator as he awaited the inevitable verdict.

Once it arrived, there was a moment of discussion between the two men at the crease, before the dismissed batter punched a dogmatic fist into his powerful forearm to form a doomed T.

The detective sighed and turned back to Mrs Alvarado. He handed back her phone.

"No," he said. "There's no need to interrogate the follower who saw the stray DM. As soon as you handed me the spreadsheet, I created an account in your name and followed @FourSeasons-FourMillionReasons."

"You did *what?*" she said. "I don't want to be on Twitter."

"Perfectly understandable," admitted the detective. "But if it's any consolation, you're *barely* on it. You have only one follower. See?"

Mrs Alvarado stared at the notification on her screen. "Who's this?" she said.

"I'm very confident that's your husband's other account," he said. "And the only way he'd know this newly created account of yours even existed would be if @FourSeasonsFourMillionReasons panicked and contacted him, telling him that his wife was following her."

On the big screen, the ball tracking confirmed three red lights. The batter was out.

"Dammit," said the detective. He turned back to Mrs Alvarado. "I've saved the relevant screen shots of your new account and who followed it and when they did so to your phone. I'm sure Gervais will be able to tie this second account to your husband. That should be enough to secure you a very decent share of his social media fortune in the divorce and ensure you and Gervais can start a happy life together."

The detective stood and began to applaud the batter as he trudged off the field. As he did so, I took the opportunity to usher Mrs Alvarado away.

"I hope you don't think that Gervais and I are doing anything indecent," she said, as we reached the bottom of the stand.

"The detective's not here to judge," I said, handing over the Square reader for the remainder of the fee. She tapped it with her credit card. "He's just here to solve mysteries during regularly scheduled breaks in cricket matches."

And thank goodness he is! Stay tuned for further baffling mysteries that can only be solved by the sleuth of slower balls, the gumshoe of googlies, the investigator of inside edges: the Tragic Detective.

GREAT CRICKETING BRAINS

After centuries of unsightly bickering, the greatest mathematical geniuses of all time and their literary counterparts have agreed to settle their fundamental differences in the most appropriate manner possible - a fifty overs per side limited overs cricket match.

TEAMS

Team selection has been riddled with controversy, with selectors of both sides mustering some surprising omissions and shock inclusions. The main point of contention was the eligibility of Werner Heisenberg for the Mathematicians team. There was a great deal of uncertainty around this point, but ultimately, the ICC (Intellectual Cricket Council) decided he was both a) more of a Physicist and b) too liable to confuse fans of *Breaking Bad* and he was ruled out.

The selectors settled upon the following teams:

Mathematicians

Pythagoras, Euclid, Newton (c), Gauss, Fibonacci, Pascal, Fermat (wk), Khayyam, Cantor, Euler, Godel

Writers

Dickens, Austen, Shakespeare (c), Wordsworth, Wilde, Milton (wk), Joyce, Hemingway, Kafka, Christie, Bronte

PLAYERS TO WATCH

The Mathematicians will hope Euclid can lay a robust foundation for their innings before their middle order is forced to face the bewildering James Joyce and mystery spinner Agatha Christie.

For the Writers, they will be once again building their innings around the bat of William Wordsworth, who has found superb rhythm and timing. Leading the Mathematician attack will be Georg Cantor, who has in recent times gone to a new level.

THE TOSS

The Writers won the toss, much to the delight of Writers captain William Shakespeare. "To bat or not to bat," he mused to

Mark Nicholas. "That is the question. Whether 'tis nobler in the contest to suffer the slings and arrows of setting a target, Or to take guard against a first innings total, And, by opposing, chase it down?"

While Shakespeare contemplated his options, Mathematicians captain Isaac Newton approached match referee David Boon to raise questions over the coin used in the toss and, in particular, what natural forces caused it to fall to the ground at all.

But any concerns over the validity of the toss were resolved by the cobbled together probability theory of Blaise Pascal and Pierre de Fermat and after Shakespeare ended his soliloquy with a determination to bat first, the game continued as scheduled.

WRITERS' INNINGS

Cantor bowled a magnificent opening spell, with the six balls in each of his opening overs containing an infinite variety of skill. It was Leonhard Euler who took the early wickets, however. Moving the ball infinitesimally off the pitch, Euler persuaded Jane Austen to play a shot lacking in sense and she was caught behind for eight.

Euler followed with the prize scalp of William Shakespeare, who had a fatally flawed moment of indecision. He uttered a brief 'Zounds!' as the ball flew off the edge to Pythagoras in the slips, who took the chance at just the right angle. Shakespeare's duck triggered much ado, as the Mathematicians wildly celebrated his wicket. Writers 20/2 in the sixth over.

Despite clearly wanting more, Charles Dickens then had to settle for a score of just 24 when Cantor removed him with a delivery that moved diagonally to take the off stump. It looked to be the worst of times for the Writers at 51/3, as Shakespeare's hopes of a power play that would reverberate throughout history was instead replaced by a comedy of errors.

But Oscar Wilde arrived at the crease, and the controversy of his selection in the team was quickly forgotten. The man known as 'Wilde Thing' played some flamboyant strokes as he proved yet again that while he may be inconsistent, he cannot be accused of being unimaginative.

However, when Omar Khayyam dropped in the short ball, Wilde could not resist the temptation to hook. He was caught at deep fine leg, only to be reprieved by a front foot no ball call.

A disappointed Khayyam retraced each step of his approach to the crease and repeated his process. Again, he dropped it short. Again, Wilde hooked. Again, Wilde was caught. This time to a legitimate delivery. Wilde fell into the trap once. But one might have expected him to take extra care the second time around. Writers 130/4 in the 24th over.

The wicket of new batter John Milton was then immediately lost, as the leg-spinner Godel turned a delivery back in on itself. Milton was trapped, and his fall from the heavenly heights he attained at the start of his career now seems unlikely to ever end.

At 135/5, William Wordsworth must have wondered whether he was playing a lone hand. But any cloudiness to his mood cleared with James Joyce's arrival to the crease. Joyce batted in typically unorthodox fashion, innovating his way to a free-wheeling half-century. Joyce is no longer a young man, but he left Wordsworth in his wake, as the innings surged past 200 in the 35th over.

The Mathematicians seemed in real trouble, but Newton knew he could count on Cantor. And so it proved, as the veteran seamer found a way through Joyce, bringing Ernest Hemingway to the crease. Hemingway shouldered arms at his first delivery and had to farewell the crease as the ball jagged back and took his off stump. 212/7 in the 38th over.

Franz Kafka's arrival at the crease seemed to invoke a metamorphosis in Wordsworth's batting and he hit out to bring up an impressive century. He lost his wicket shortly after, however, to leave the Writers 252/8 in the 46th over.

There were no specialists at the crease. Instead, the mystery of how best to resolve the death overs fell to Agatha Christie, who, despite her vast experience, had no answers. 257/9

Some late hitting from Kafka and Emily Bronte, however, saw the Writers finish on 286/9 from their fifty overs. The Mathematicians conferred and between them soon had an irrefutable proof that they needed 287 runs for victory.

MATHEMATICIANS' INNINGS

The old firm of Pythagoras and Euclid opened the batting for the Mathematicians, facing the pace attack of Bronte and Dickens. Both struck early boundaries, with their angled bats bisecting the field with ease.

But Dickens rapidly lived up to expectations, catching the edge of Pythagoras's bat. 23/1 in the third over.

Isaac Newton came to the crease and misjudged a slower ball from Bronte. Newton's bat, already in motion, stayed in motion, and he skied the delivery from Bronte to great heights before it dropped inevitably back into the bowler's hands. 25/2 after four overs.

Dickens continued to weave a tale of misery for the Mathematicians. He showed he was Euclid-proof, as he prevented the experienced opener from scoring, before eventually dismissing him. 31/3 off seven overs.

Fibonacci joined Gauss at the crease and made scoring shots of 1, 1, 2 and 3. But the introduction of spin in the form of the cocky Kafka saw him dismissed. 48/4 in the twelfth over.

Any hope that Pascal had of adding to the previous batters' scores were soon dashed. He was instead out for four, also falling to Kafka, who was proving a trial for the Mathematician batters. 55/5. The Mathematicians now needed something truly remarkable from Fermat, who was theoretically their last chance to salvage something from the run chase. Instead, his innings barely deserved a note in a margin as he became Joyce's first victim, caught behind for just nine to leave the Mathematicians 67/6 in the nineteenth over.

This brought Khayyam came to the crease, and his methodical process for dealing with the Writers' bowlers led to reliable outcomes.

He and Gauss added 80 to the total, both surviving a long, difficult to read, spell from Joyce. Gauss, in particular, imposed order on the apparent randomness of Joyce, bringing up his fifty off a mere 46 deliveries, despite batting normally.

Shakespeare introduced Christie into the attack and she struck Khayyam on the pads first ball. The entire Writers team went up for the appeal. "Out, out!" wailed Shakespeare. "Damned spot!" he went on to exclaim, as his review was turned down thanks to a clear mark on the inside edge.

Khayyam's reprieve didn't last long, however, and he fell not long after to Hemingway. It had been Wilde, fielding at cover, who suggested to his captain the importance of bowling Ernest. Hemingway also rose to the challenge, the man and the old seam combining to dismiss Khayyam for 26 (47). The wicket reduced the Mathematicians to 151/7, still requiring 136 runs from 93 balls, with just three wickets in hand.

The identity of the next batter turned out to be Euler, promoted in the order. He joined Gauss, and the pair added a further 64 off the next six overs before Wilde, fielding at point, ran out the tail-ender as he scrambled for a non-existent single. "There is only one thing worse than being run out for 36," offered Wilde in consolation. "And that's not being run out for 36."

Cantor came to the crease, and he began a search for a realistic path to victory, carefully counting down both the runs remaining and balls required.

But with the dismissal of Gauss, caught in the deep by Hemingway for a magnificent 121 (95), the bell had finally seemed to toll for the Mathematicians.

At 270/9, with two overs remaining, it was clear to almost everybody that the last wicket partnership would need seventeen runs for victory off twelve balls. But the new batter Godel showed this wasn't guaranteed to be the case. Indeed, Godel came up with a proof that the fundamental axioms of arithmetic were not necessarily consistent. As a result, nobody could be certain that *either* side could attain victory in a traditional additive sense.

Godel's proof proved too difficult to follow for most, however, and in the end, it was Cantor who ended up stumped.

By Milton, off the bowling of Joyce.

Shakespeare's Writers had won. All's well that ends well.

THREE TEAM CRICKET

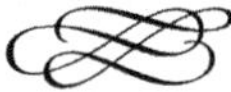

In July, 2020, mid-pandemic, South Africa held the Solidarity Cup, a magnificent innovation in the sport that heralded the introduction of its greatest form - 3 Team Cricket. Here's my report card from that match.

Three Team Cricket (3TCricket) is here! Those geniuses in South Africa have bloody well cracked it, transforming cricket from a pathetic two team sport that we've foolishly loved all these years, only because we lacked the vision to ponder 'what if there was a third team in the mix?'

Cricket South Africa didn't ponder. They went ahead and did it, without giving a tinker's cuss what anybody else might have thought. They know that 3TCricket doesn't care about rules or schemas. It's a free spirit, not beholden to this modern database-driven world. It gives the finger to Silicon Valley by adding to the mix an extra team, hill fishermen, Makhaya Ntini having the time of his life and whatever the hell else it pleases.

Here's my report card for the inaugural 3TCricket match, the Solidarity Cup between The Eagles, The Kites and The Kingfishers

ENGLAND V WEST INDIES - GRADE: D+

The England v West Indies Test was the only other form of cricket being televised around the world. Naturally, realising how absurd their silly little two-team cricket match would look when compared to the majesty of 3TCricket, the ECB conspired to have the entire day of the Test washed out. An understandable retreat.

On the other hand, the Solidarity Cup was *sponsored by rain*. It's like the old judo trick of turning your opponent's strengths against them. Cricket South Africa, take a bow.

The ECB, however, cannot continue to have days of the Test rained out just to avoid embarrassment at being upstaged by 3TCricket. That's not a sustainable ploy. At some point they'll have to resume the Test mach, no matter how ridiculous they feel playing such a self-evidently inferior form of the game.

If the ECB have any sense whatsoever they'll take note and realise that Pakistan are already over there. It's not too late to corral them into the dugout, awaiting their turn in the third innings. You try to tell me there's not a team better suited for 3TCricket than Pakistan. You can't, can you?

THE RULES - GRADE: A-

Before the match began, we had the welcome sight of Mark Nicholas Zooming in from England to tell us how simple the rules are in this three team format. And, of course they are. It's a straightforward rotating cyclical two-team match-up first half, randomly generated, as all three teams move through the classic batting, bowling and dugout phases of the match.

Then the second half has a reverse-cyclical match-up sorted in batting order from highest-to-lowest first half scores, with the innings resuming from where it left off, until all three teams are resorted onto the podium according to who finishes with the most runs overall.

There are other fresh elements in the mix, such as the 'last man standing' rule where, after the seventh batter is dismissed, the last batter in gets to bat on, by himself. (Did I mention there are only eight players per team? Because there are, of course.)

The last batter is, however, only allowed to score in multiples of two. Except, presumably, from the last ball of the over. This was an aspect of the game that had Nicholas most excited - he was looking forward to the gladiatorial prospects of the last man standing and I, for one, was not inclined to argue with him. I would have given anything to see AB de Villiers batting with a net and trident. Alas, it was not to be. Although we came closer than anybody might reasonably have expected.

THE FIRST HALF - GRADE: B+

As always in 3TCricket, the first half is a sizing up exercise. One wants to stay in touch with the other two teams, but not necessarily be the top run-scorer, as this means you bat first in the second half, a position fraught with peril.

The Kingfishers - dressed as super-villain Lex Luthor for no immediately obvious reason - made 2/56 batting first. The Eagles - led by super-Villiers, AB de Luthor - then took a ten run lead, before the Kites slotted into the tactically desirable middle-run position, finishing on 58 from their opening six overs. A classic 3TCricket first half. One for the true fans.

The eight run lead going into the second half gave the Eagles the opportunity to put the game out of reach. They knew they'd be bowling in the final innings, which meant - obviously - that if the Kites didn't run them down in the second third of the second half, the Eagles bowlers would have the game in their hands.

The Kites, on the other hand, were incentivised to limit the Eagles scoring first up in the second half, to hopefully allow their batters to take the lead and then rely on the Eagles to earn themselves a consolation silver medal by curtailing the Kingfishers run chase.

And, of course, the Kingfishers would be bowling second and batting last, so they would know exactly what to do in the second half. A great position to be in, assuming the other two teams (particularly the Eagles with their ten(!) run head start) didn't pull too far away.

Just a standard 3TCricket strategic day at the office.

NTINIS - GRADE: A+

Despite the natural caution we've come to expect from a 3TCricket first half, as teams feel one another out, there was no shortage of thrills.

For one thing, there were ball boys on the hill with a net to catch sixes. These hill fishermen added another magnificent element to the game, celebrating wildly as they caught the ball behind their backs. It is, however, perhaps a missed opportunity. What if the dugout team were employed in the classic cricket role of hill fishermen? Maybe they could also score six runs for their team if they caught the ball with the net. Now, *that's* a fresh tactical dimension to consider. I assume that'll be a rule for the next match, such is the dizzying and welcome speed of 3TCricket innovation.

Also, the next match will no doubt be commentated solely by Makhaya Ntini, who absolutely bossed the commentary box. He cheered everything that happened, roaring with delight at the delicious madness that surrounded every aspect of this thrilling new format. Not least of which was his own son's bowling, which climaxed with guffaws of laughter when Little Ntini dropped a skied caught and bowled that the cameraman completely lost track of. It was a wild ride. Not only should 3TCricket be dominated by Ntini's commentary going forward, *all* cricket should henceforth be Makhaya Ntini commentating on his son's bowling.

THE SECOND HALF - GRADE: A

The second half began with the Eagles, via Markram and de Villiers, teeing off. Markram racked up yet another 3TCricket half-century. What a consistent performer he is at this level.

AB de Villiers followed him shortly thereafter as the Eagles smashed their way to 4/160. The huge total looked to have put the game out of reach for the Kites and Kingfishers. Still, as the old saying goes, 'whatever they score in the first third of the second half we can score in the second or third third of the second half (plus the first half score gap)'.

But it proved to be a bridge too far. The Kites went for it, knowing they'd be in the dugout for the final innings. The dreaded 'Dugout At The Death' slot. Nobody wants it but one side always has it. That's the beauty of 3TCricket. Nevertheless, they fell 22 runs short, finishing on 3/138.

The Kingfishers needed 103 from their second half six overs to win. An enormous task, but fearless Faf du Plessis didn't back away from the chase. He came to the crease, determined to go for the gold medal. That's what you love to see in 3TCricket. Alas, however, he was dismissed by some fool bowler who cares not for a Faf Dash for Gold, and the Kingfishers stumbled instead to a bronze medal, finishing on 5/113.

A comprehensive win and/or second place finish. Probably a good thing. If the match had been close in any way, my head might have exploded in excitement. Still, a magnificent game of 3TCricket. Congratulations to all three teams for a podium finish.

I can’t wait for the next one.

YOU SAY YOU WANT A RESOLUTION

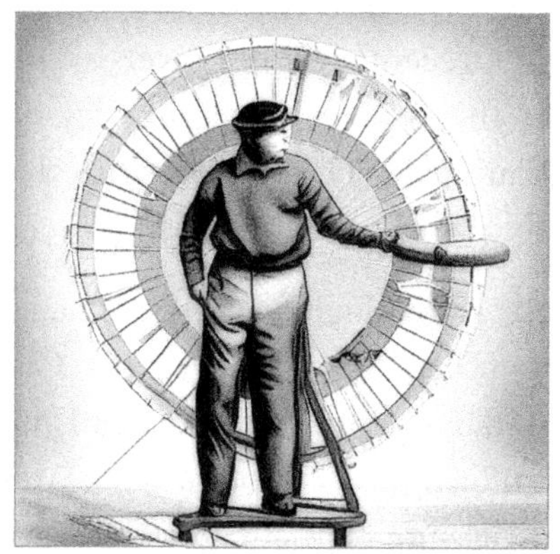

A shorter version of this piece was originally published in the 2020 ABC Cricket Guide. *Luckily for you, I've expanded it with extra nonsense.*

Nothing is quite as unsatisfying as a sporting contest that has no outright winner. There's a vague emptiness at the heart of these evenly-matched outcomes. We don't play sport just so that we can conclude 'yeah, we're both pretty good, eh?'. We compete to determine a winner.

And yet there are many occasions when the cricket itself doesn't supply a victor, forcing us to call upon other methods to determine who claims the match and/or series and/or tournament. And that's where the problems begin.

(A case can be made for letting Test match draws be. Draws are a beloved aspect of the game, which have given cricket fans some of their most treasured memories, and there's no reason whatsoever to change them. After all, who can forget Faf du Plessis defying Peter Siddle in Adelaide, 2012 for most of the final day? Or Glenn McGrath and Brett Lee seeing out the last four overs of the Third Test of the 2005 Ashes? Or the summer when the lifeless Perth track drove Mitchell Johnson to give up on the game entirely? Wonderful moments in the game. It would be madness to discard the draw. Tied Test matches can, however, get in the recently-kicked-over-by-Justin Langer bin. We've had two of them so far in the history of Tests. Two too many by my reckoning. Sort out a system for declaring a winner before an inevitable third tie shows up.)

But it's not just individual matches that cause problems. England were awarded an actual World Cup because they struck more boundaries than New Zealand in the final, a feat equivalent to them facing more dot balls. (It is, after all, virtually impossible to tie a one day international by scoring more boundaries without simultaneously facing more dot balls. That's just how arithmetic works.) And a limited overs trophy being awarded to a side for playing out more scoreless deliveries feels wrong.

In that same English summer, Australia retained the Ashes by dint of having won them in the previous series. This trophy-deciding methodology at least has the benefit of 140-odd years of tradition. Also, it means that, in retrospect, Steve Smith won the 2019 Ashes not just with his 774 runs in 2019 but also his

687 runs in 2017/18. Scoring 1461 runs at 121.75 to win an Ashes series? Suck on that, Bradman.

There are other methods of resolving ties but they're not satisfying either. Australia famously progressed ahead of South Africa in the tied 1999 World Cup semi-final because of net run rate, a concept that's only fully understood by hardcore nerds. And, as we saw in the previously mentioned 2019 World Cup final, Super Overs are fundamentally flawed because they're even easier to tie than the original match.

Furthermore, a problem common to all these tie-breaking methods is that one team goes into them knowing they have to do less than the other. Australia could retain the Ashes by winning the same number of Tests as England. England could win the World Cup by scoring the same number of runs as New Zealand in the Super Over.

Wouldn't it be fairer if the method for splitting a tied result was decided only *after* the tie itself? It would certainly make both teams strive harder for the win.

So why not spin a wheel of possible tie-breaking methodologies and then use the result from that spin to determine the result of the match?

The wheel could have all the classic tie-breakers - net run rate, most boundaries, whoever won it last time - but it could also have new concepts as well, limited only by our imaginations. Fewest dot balls faced? Put it on the wheel. Best use of DRS? Put it on the wheel. Handsomest fast bowling captain? Oh, Pat Cummins, you'd better believe we're putting that on the wheel.

And once you've got this wheel being used for tournaments and Test series, why not go further and use the same wheel spin approach to decide future tied Tests as well?

Imagine if the 1986 tied Test had been decided by the wheel landing on a 'player most soaked in their own urine' slot. Now you've got a true reward for Dean Jones' legendarily dehydrated heroics in that match. Or what if Richie Benaud and Frank Worrell had raced to be the one that hits the Super Six that ends and wins the Test? That's how you make a tied Test memorable.

I see a match ending with scores level and the presentation ceremony beginning, with the result still up in the air. A neutral official (eg the match referee or former Big Bash mascot Gus the Goose) would then spin the wheel and determine a tie-breaking methodology. Any necessary calculations for the chosen tie-breaker (for example, the computation of net run rate or checking the results of a Twitter poll) would then be performed live on air. Once completed, the official would then cut off their tie with scissors to symbolically indicate the tie being formally broken. And, finally, a satisfying and fair winner of the Test match/Test series/Big Bash/World Cup would be celebrated.

Now, that's what I call cricket.

MR WARNER

Once upon a tour, there was a man called Mr Warner.

Mr Warner was very bored. Here he was in Africa, and the only lion he'd seen was his off-spinner, Mr Lyon.

And he wasn't interesting to anybody.

So Mr Warner approached his captain, Mr Smith. Mr Smith was hard at work in his workshop, working out new ways to make runs.

"I've just had a great idea of how to make this tour more interesting," said Mr Warner.

"I don't have time to listen," said Mr Smith, hammering away at his bench. "But you'd warn me if it was going to get us into trouble, right?"

"Of course I would," said Mr Warner. "After all, I'm Mr Warner."

But what Mr Smith didn't know was that Mr Warner's name was deeply ironic.

The next thing anybody knew, Mr Warner and Mr Smith were banned for a year.

"Ouch!" said Mr Smith.

"I think that's my call to action," said Mr Paine.

It was. And everybody lived happily ever after.

(As long as everybody stuck to the story...)

THE LAST QUESTION

One last question before we go, mate.

Sure.

Which cricketer would you pick to bat for your life?

To what?

To bat for your life.

… in what sense?

Uh, y'know, in the sense that, if your life depended on it, who would you want at the crease.

If my *life* depended on it?

Sure. Who do you think would handle the pressure the best?

I would simply refuse to place myself in such a ludicrously risky scenario. I mean, what's the upside to this?

Well, there isn't one. It's more, like, a hypothetical. A thought experiment.

A thought experiment? No, no, no. A thought experiment is a philosophical examination of the underpinnings of a particular known state, so that we can explore its logical ramifications and, in doing so, perhaps challenge our preconceptions. What preconceptions are we challenging here? The danger inherent in having my ongoing existence inexorably tied to the ability of a cricketer to not lose their wicket? I feel as if that's already *extremely* well established.

But that's kind of the point. Who would you most trust to not *lose their wicket under that pressure? You know, like a, say, Steve Waugh or—*

Steve Waugh? What in blazes makes you think that Steve Waugh cares one iota about my life? Of all the characteristics historically associated with the former Australian captain - his determination, his bloody-mindedness, his ruthlessness - you're ascribing to the top tier his unbounded *empathy*?

Okay, fine. Then what about, say, Rahul Dravid? The Wall.

Dravid?! Dravid batted 605 times in international cricket and lost his wicket on 533 occasions. Am I supposed to be happy with a 12% chance of surviving this preposterous scenario?

Okay, not Dravid either. You can choose whoever you like.

Look, to even *begin* to decide which batter I'd entrust with this macabre responsibility, I'd need far more information on how the entire process works.

Like what? Which bowlers they'll face?

Who cares what bowlers they're facing? The odds are overwhelmingly against me, regardless. Unless, y'know, the whole thing is a pointlessly mismatched charade.

So what do *you need to know?*

The mechanics of the entire thing. I mean, how, exactly, is the loss of my life tied to the loss of the wicket? Is it like a zing bail thing?

I dunno. Maybe.

Because if it is, perhaps I can find a cricketer with some kind of training in electrical circuitry. Or an apprentice sparky. Anybody who, in between deliveries, might be able to dismantle the underpinning mechanism that ties our fates together.

I'm not sure that's quite in the spirit of the—

Or failing that, get Watto out there to stick his enormous front pad in front of anything that came his way.

Well, I don't think that would save you. LBW would have to count for the purposes of the experiment.

Okay. So then it's *not* a zing bail thing?

I guess not.

Is it an umpire thing? Is it triggered by the raising of their finger? Because surely even the most rigid and unflinching of officials would curb their zeal for giving a batter out if it was simply explained to them the gruesome ramifications of their strict adherence to the Laws of the game.

Perhaps.

Perhaps? They'd have to be a sociopath to behave otherwise, surely. They're caught in the middle of this as surely as I am. Would they really prefer to have an innocent person's death on their conscience?

Probably not. But—

Do I get reviews? Because if the batter is given out by a psycho-pathic umpire so dogmatically determined to end the life of an otherwise-unconnected third party, I'd really prefer for them to not make a mistake.

I'm sure you'd get a review.

Great. So if the onfield umpires remain, despite all appeals to their better nature, willing to be accessories to my murder, I can still attempt to reason with the third umpire?

I guess.

Or I could hire somebody to hack into the various systems - the ball-tracking, the edge detection and so forth - and edit the data on the fly to ensure the batter survives, thus ensuring my own ongoing survival.

That sounds tricky.

Of course it does. It's *Mission Impossible*-style bullshit. But this is quite literally a life and death situation for me. I will be exploring all avenues, no matter how unlikely to succeed, in order to disentangle my destiny from that of the batter.

I really think you're thinking too much about this.

If you think I'm thinking about it too much, maybe you'd like to swap places in this insane death trap.

Fine.

Great.

(The interview subject removes the electrified helmet from his head and places it on the journalist, who is horrified to hear David Warner almost immediately trapped plumb in front by Stuart Broad. The journalist lets out a small scream as his skull is fried by the ensuing powerful electrical shock. The interview subject goes to the whiteboard and puts an emphatic line through David Warner's name.)

CRYPTIC CROSSWORD 2

OPENERS

Across

1 This seamer is back with some truths, laws and consequences (5)

5 The best test result of a fluid diet (4)

8 Bowl unchanged, heading in to the break (5)

10 Need to hang on to one that's flying or else you're undismissable (5,4,3)

13 Condemn an innings (5)

14 Did you see Mendis miss a leg-cutter? In or out? (9)

16 Liking the newness of the ball (5)

20 Have Australia yet discarded every negative opener? (6)

21 "Is he the top of the order?" foul vulgarians ask (5,8)

23 Opening the batting? Nope. (7)

24 This fielder first saw a century take six balls (5)

25 A good start to an innings upsets a regal end (4,5)

27 He's back as the tail score runs (6)

29 Swing bowler in the channel, I hear (6)

30 Strangely, he led a Kiwi bowling attack (6)

31 A very short innings, but not out (2)

33 The bowler saw a mark, I'm discovering (5,5)

35 The all-rounder has a place in the side, I hear, that wily devil (5,3)

37 On a half century, for example (3)

38 The all-rounder had hair, but only after it was cut back (7)

40 See 35A

41 A batting line-up free of chaos (5)

42 With some R&D, a great opener could span nations, eras and sexes?

Down

2 1A's partner means AB's more bruised (7)

3 I hear he made a mess of batters (5)

4 He's just learning and evolving (6,6)

5 He's possibly not Buttler (5,5)

6 Bob makes a quick trip to the middle (4)

7 Carry on with the gasps of admiration about the ton from this captain (5)

9 The seamer had a vain scam break down (8,4)

11 A single use (3)

12 Between overs, television viewers see the first sign of Allan Donald (2)

15 The keeper is in? Ha! All say 'yes' (6,5)

17 Edged? Gone? Or grin crazily, because he's still batting? (6,9)

18 The number one player is back on it (4)

19 Unusually, I am both an adept batter and bowler (3,6)

22 China's erratic batter (6)

25 Talk about ceasing play (11)

26 Cricket ball fan (3)

28 Something about the new ball is the same, but different (4)

31 Recklessly rank him an all-rounder without peer (5,4)

32 The captain can adapt on the radio (6)

34 Within a proper boundary (4)

36 Brett's baby? (6)

39 It's not the end of the match? (4)

THE SADDEST SIX WORD CRICKET STORY

For sale: baby leggie, never Warne

LOCK-DON

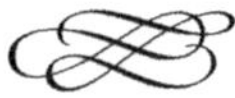

SEASON 1, EPISODE 2

T*he pilot of Lock-Don was an unfathomable success and, as a result, it went to series.*

'Breakfast Breakthrough'

FADE IN:

INT. KITCHEN - MORNING

THE DON is at the stove, making an omelette. His spatula work is swift, clinical and precise. The eggs do not stand a chance. LOCK wanders in, dressed in loose pyjama pants and a stain-riddled 'Teenage Mutant Ninja Turtles' T-shirt.

THE DON
(cheerily)
Good morning, sleepyhead! Would you like an omelette?

LOCK, still half-asleep, grunts in reply, then spots a completed jigsaw puzzle on the kitchen table.

LOCK
Oh, come on! You finished it? I thought we were going to work on it together.

THE DON
I know. But I started it this morning, and practically without exception every piece went where it was intended. Before I knew it, I was done. Easily my finest jigsaw puzzle.

THE DON hands LOCK a mug of black coffee. LOCK thumps it down, splashing coffee on the COMPLETED JIGSAW, which we now see is a photo of THE DON making 254 at Lord's in 1930.

LOCK
(frustrated)
Well, if we're not going to work on the jigsaw together, I think we should order a Nintendo Switch. Then we could play that hit game everybody's talking about, *Animal Crossing*.

THE DON
Come on, Tony. You know my feelings on Switch hits.

The simulated studio audience guffaws, as we segue into THE OPENING CREDITS. As the last notes of the LOCK-DON THEME SONG fade away, LOCK resumes his case.

LOCK
Seriously, we should look at getting this game. I was on a Zoom call with Kallis and Hobbs last night--

THE DON
(interrupting)
You shouldn't humour him like that. You know that Hobbs isn't really there. It's just a stuffed Jack Hobbs toy that Kallis likes to pretend is alive.

LOCK
And what's the harm in that? I had a stuffed Jack Hobbs growing up and he was my best friend.
(remembering his point)
Anyway, they have a Nintendo Switch and they've been playing *Animal Crossing*. Hobbs has built an entire community of tigers, but there are all kinds of animals in the game.

THE DON
Are there ducks? The last thing I want to see are ducks.

The simulated studio audience understands the reference and goes 'ooo-oooh'.

LOCK
I'm pretty sure there are ducks.

THE DON
Then why are we bothering with it? Let's just play Test Match Cricket.

THE DON gestures to the end of the kitchen bench, where they have the classic TEST MATCH CRICKET game set up. The plastic spring-loaded bowler is ready to bowl and the equally plastic fielders are positioned haphazardly on the GREEN FELT OUTFIELD.

LOCK
I'm bored with Test Match Cricket.

THE DON
That's only because I'm 0/309.

The simulated studio audience breaks into sustained simulated applause.

LOCK
(under his breath)
309/0.
(shaking his head)
And no, that's not it. I'm just sick of that particular game.

THE DON
Then what about Armchair Cricket? Wicketz? Dice Cricket?

LOCK

No, no and no. You win all of those too. You win every game we play.

THE DON

I don't win *every* game.

(hesitates)

Maybe just 95% of them.

LOCK

(suddenly angry)

You think I win even 5% of the games we play? No way. Trust me, mate, I know what 1 in 20 looks like. 1 in 20 is *fantastic*. I've always said that. But I don't win *any* games against you, and I'm sick of it. It's not all about you, Donald.

THE DON

Now, now. There's no need for cross words, Tony. Unless, that is, you want to try this.

He tosses a folded over newspaper to LOCK.

THE DON (CONT'D)

I only just started the cryptic crossword after I finished the jigsaw. There are still a few clues left to complete.

LOCK

(looking at a clue)

Okay, let's see. '19 Down: Dons a tattered armband (7)'

Hmmm... 'tattered' sounds like an anagram indicator.

(he checks the grid)

First letter, B. Last letter, n.

(muttering)

Oh, you've got to be kidding me.

Some members of the simulated studio audience titter as they catch on. LOCK tosses the newspaper across the room.

THE DON
What's the matter?

LOCK
Even the bloody crossword is all about you.
(he emits a frustrated sigh)
How's that omelette going?

THE DON
Almost done.

LOCK
Why does it take so long? I was Skyping with Harold and Douglas yesterday and they said they've been working on something called 'fast egg theory'.

THE DON
(to himself)
That's not what I call it.

LOCK
Douglas said that sometimes you crack a few more eggs than most people would like, but the results are worth it in the end.

THE DON wanders over from the stove and places an omelette in front of LOCK and a piece of paper beside him. The paper has a line drawn down the middle. On the left side is written 'Donald'. On the other side is 'Tony', with at least FIFTY TALLY MARKS beneath it.

LOCK
(looking at the paper)
What's this?

THE DON
That's a tally of all the games we've played, and who lost each one. Look, you're thrashing me!

The simulated studio audience explodes with uproarious laughter. They applaud enthusiastically.

LOCK
I guess that'll have to do.

END CREDITS ROLL

LOCK
(in between bites of his omelette)
But I still want a Nintendo Switch.

EXCERPT FROM 'UGL(Y AUSS)IES' BY SCOTT WESTERFELD

Scott Westerfeld is a Young Adult fiction author, whose best-selling 'Ugl(y Auss)ies' trilogy imagines a dystopian future where all Australian cricketers are forced to shed their unpleasant exterior.

CHAPTER ONE

Tim was an Ugly Aussie.

But not for much longer. Soon he would undergo the operation that converted him from one of the Ugly Aussies - Uglies for short - to a socially acceptable member of world cricket.

He wondered what he would become once Cricket Australia completed their operation. Would he become an Applauder, politely clapping when opposition players reached milestones? A Clarifier, helping the umpires out by letting them know that catches hadn't carried? Or maybe, just maybe, he might become...

No. He refused to allow himself to even hope that he might become a Walker. He was just plain old Tim, from Tasmania.

Even once he was filled with the Spirit of Cricket, he couldn't possibly become something as noble as a Walker.

But what if he did?

He imagined himself edging a ball to the keeper in a World Cup Semi-Final, the umpire saying 'not out' and then walking off the ground anyway.

The crowd would applaud him all the way to the dressing room. Commentators would heap praise on his choice. Maybe even the umpire might give him a little clap.

'That Tim,' they would say. 'He's not one of the Ugly Aussies.'

So caught up was he in the daydream that he didn't even notice the shadowy figure that had suddenly appeared beside him.

"Daydreaming about the operation, are we?" the figure suddenly said in a growling voice that seemed to teeter always on the brink of a swear word.

"No, I was just..." began Tim. But he didn't know what to say next.

"You're standing outside the Sutherland Laboratories, with that dopey look on your face. I've seen it a million times before. You're daydreaming." He spat violently. "I'm Matty, by the way."

"I'm Tim," he replied, offering his hand to shake.

Matty ignored it. "I know who you are," said Matty. "And I know you're counting the days until you get The Spirit injected into you during the operation."

"And what if I am?" said Tim, suddenly angry. "What's wrong with that?"

The question was met with a snort from Matty, and a question of his own in response. "Do you really want to know?" he said.

And without understanding why, Tim found himself saying yes.

MATTY LED TIM TO 'THE SLEDGE', WHICH HE EXPLAINED WAS A renegade settlement where Ugly Aussies fled to avoid the operation.

"Why wouldn't you want to have the operation?" asked Tim. "Don't you care about the culture of Australian cricket?"

"Do you even know *why* we're forced to have the operation?" asked Matty.

Tim had heard the legends. Of the ball that was tampered with. The crotch that hid the sandpaper. The public outcry. The lengthy bans. The tearful press conferences.

Everybody had heard these legends. Everybody knew that was why the operation had been set up. To once and for all put an end to Ugly Aussies and the embarrassment that invariably came with them.

He told Matty all of this.

Matty just laughed.

"You're a wicket-keeper, aren't you Tim?" asked Matty.

"Yes," said Tim.

"Then you, of all people, deserve to know the truth," said Matty. "You see, the operation doesn't just remove the part of us that makes us Ugly Aussies. It also removes our mongrel. And good old-fashioned Aussie mongrel is what sets us apart."

"But we've been spoken to by the Cricket Australia scientists," said Tim. "They told us that the procedure was perfectly harmless to our cricketing prowess. That, if anything, the Spirit of Cricket injection would make us *better* cricketers."

Matty shook his head sadly. "That's just not true, Tim," he said. "Have you ever seen an Australian cricketer who'd undergone the operation?"

Tim nodded quietly.

"Then you'll have noticed they have no presence," said Matty. "Because the sad fact is you can't remove what makes us Ugly Aussies without removing everything about us that makes us special. Cricket Australia knows that perfectly well, but they keep it a secret. Because they don't want the Ugly Aussies to ever embarrass them again."

Tim gasped. "But that's terrible," he said. He thought for a moment. "What can we do about this?" he eventually asked.

"That's what we wanted to talk to you about," said Matty.

"'We'?" said Tim.

"Yes," said Matty. And as he said it, three more figures emerged from the shadows. Matty pointed to each in turn as he introduced them. "This is Ian. Over there is Bradley. And that one with beer running down his moustache is Rodney."

Tim gave an uncomfortable wave. "Hello," he said. All three responded with an onslaught of abuse.

"We're the Keepers," said Matty. "We're the Ugliest Aussies of them all. And we want you, Tim, to destroy Cricket Australia and its operation from the inside."

Tim stared, wide-eyed.

"Now," said Matty. "Can I offer you a pickle juice?"

TAKING T20S INTO THE '20S… AND BEYOND

Originally published in the 2020 ABC Cricket Guide, *the brief was a light-hearted piece on whether the T20 format wants to be taken more seriously, or less.*

What's the future of T20s? More and more, teams are hiring nerds to analyse Expected Averages (EAs), True Strike Rates (TSRs), Pitch Ratings (PRs) and other Acronymified Cricket Measures (ACMs) in an attempt to finally elevate cricket to where it's always yearned to be - a mathematically optimised algorithm for bat-and-ball sporting excellence.

But even as the analysts push T20s into deeply rigorous analytical territory, international boards tinker with the format to make it more accessible to the casual fan. And by 'more accessible to the casual fan', I mostly mean 'shorter'. England are the chief culprits here, morphing T20 into an entirely new format - The Hundred - in which bowlers bowl ten ball overs, batters score bonus runs for hitting the television drone, captains are permitted to switch out bowlers mid-over and teams are dressed up as branded packets of chips. (Only one of these is a fabrication. Can *you* guess which one?)

This is the tension that T20 will struggle with going forward - is it a serious form of the game deserving precise and detailed analysis? Or is it an entertainment vehicle existing solely to keep our minds off... well, off everything else in the world.

To quote a wise child actor from a celebrated advertisement for taco kits, why not both?

Here's how to do it: Half-T20. The exact same rules as a traditional T20 but with one crucial difference: After exchanging team sheets, we skip the toss and instead both captains bid on a target they believe they can chase. The team that bids higher gets to bat, while the underbidding captain defends the total.

Replacing the boring first innings of a T20 with a battle of wits between two captains going back and forth on potential targets accomplishes a number of goals.

Firstly, we reclaim extra time for sponsors to exploit, always important in this commercially driven age.

More importantly, we can make the auction process an event in itself. Who wouldn't love to see the crowd cheer as Aaron Finch performed an elaborate 'No Deal' gesture to an opposing captain's bid? Kids, meanwhile, could be kept entertained by special guest celebrities (for example, a bucketheaded Bachelorette or one of the Hemsworths dressed as a packet of Doritos) offering their opinions on whether the captains should bid higher. Or maybe the celebrities could just have green slime dropped on them. The point is that with the elimination of an entire innings, you'd have plenty of time to explore all entertainment options and find what appeals most to the casual cricket fan.

In addition, the entire auction process would offer fresh new mathematical areas for the boffins to analyse. Bluffing, double-bluffing, brinkmanship, mumbling your bid. So many game theory areas to explore.

And then after that, you get the run chase, with all the traditional T20 cricket and associated CricViz number-crunching anybody could ever ask for.

As the celebrated philosopher and Avengers villain Thanos the Mad Titan has taught us, sometimes less is more. The key to the future of T20 lies in getting rid of half of it.

CATCHES GENUINELY WIN MATCHES

AN IDEA FOR FIXING CRICKET MATCHES

PROBLEM WITH CURRENT LAW

It's a known cricketing fact that 'catches win matches' and yet any given cricket match can be won without a single catch being taken by the victorious side.

PROPOSED SOLUTION

In order for a side to claim victory in a cricket match, the final wicket taken must be a catch.

IMPLEMENTATION

For the team bowling last, the only way of officially winning the match is to take the tenth wicket via a catch. If the tenth wicket is taken by any other mode of dismissal, then the match is declared a draw.

For the team batting last, they win the match by surpassing their opponent's target, but *only if* the most recent wicket taken in the match is a catch. Again, if they surpass the total and the most recent wicket was some other form of dismissal, then the match will be declared a draw.

PROS

- 'Catches win matches' lives up to its promise as the great rhyming cricket truism, leaving the other candidates ('tosses inspire losses', 'run rates create fun mates', 'keepers lose peepers', 'elbow double joints cause LBWs', etcetera) shamefaced by their relative factual inaccuracy
- Ensures close finishes to virtually every match, as follows:

1. As a team closes in on a winning target while batting, they will be desperate to have a batter dismissed caught and will slow down their run-scoring until that happens. This ensures close finishes in matches that would, under current Laws, be a comfortable stroll to the winning target. Even with only a handful of runs needed to win, runs will stop and the bowling team will eventually take wickets in other ways until the ninth wicket. At that point, the tactical cat and mouse ('*catch* and mouse'? No) game begins
2. The batting side wants to lose their *ninth* wicket to a catch so they can chase the last few runs needed for a win. The bowling side needs to take the *tenth* wicket by a catch in order to win, but they know that if they take the ninth wicket by any other method, the batting side *cannot* win and hence will be incentivised to simply tread on their stumps and claim a draw. The bowling team should therefore *also* strive to take the ninth

wicket via a catch so that the tenth wicket pair can attempt to score the winning runs and potentially be caught in doing so.

3. Conversely, a bowling team that is on the brink of bowling a side out well short of their target can be undone by a series of batters stepping on their stumps to ensure the draw. Bowlers could respond by not appealing or bowling no balls, but the stalemate is ultimately most easily broken by allowing the tail to score enough runs to close in on the target, then taking the provided ninth wicket catch that opens up the possibility of victory to both sides. Again, a comfortable win is transformed into a thrilling finish.

- Catches become a more tactically compelling form of dismissal. No more is it simply enough for an athletic fielder to take a stunning grab that shows off their physical prowess, they must also prudently weigh the implications of their extraordinary hand-eye co-ordination. A brilliant reflex grab may be instantly regretted ("You cannot do that Ben Stokes") as it opens the opportunity for victory to the batting side
- First wicket partnerships become far more valuable, particularly in small run chases. If the last wicket taken in the penultimate innings is a catch, the opening pair can simply run the target down if good enough
- Introduces 'draws' to limited overs cricket

CONS

- Retired batters mess the whole thing up. Probably best to force batters to continue no matter how injured or inept they are

- A whole heap of Spirit of Cricket nonsense would almost certainly arise around catches and when it is morally right or wrong to hang onto a chance. (This may be a Pro)
- Classic Catches segments may struggle for content

FURTHER NOTES

The ninth wicket becomes the key to the match's conclusion. Under optimal play from both sides, it will be a catch that leaves the game evenly poised with a gettable target for the final two batters at the crease, but with no room for error.

In this way, the number eleven will almost always be called upon to bat with the match result resting on their hopeless shoulders. Cricket at its very best.

DAILY HOROSCOPE FOR CRICKETERS

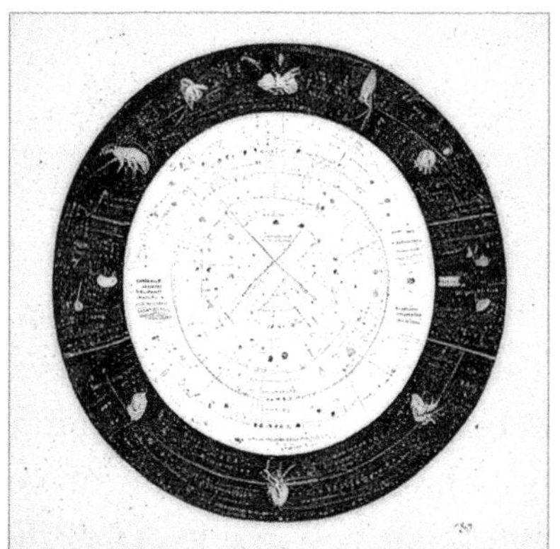

ARIES

Either your left-arm opening fast bowler or a team physiotherapist is likely to be irritable today, Aries, which might tempt you into trying to unravel their problems. But what if their problems are profound philosophical ones that have defied history's greatest thinkers for countless eons? Do you even know where to begin in diverting the path of a trolley?

It's much more complicated than pulling a single lever. Best just to stay out of it.

TAURUS

Too many balls drifting onto the batter's pads may have you feeling pressured, Taurus, creating unnecessary stress. Try to ignore it and clear your head between overs, perhaps by imagining a reboot of *House* as a weekly medical mystery show where critical diagnoses were eventually made by an actual house. No need to waste precious screen time trying to motivate Dr House's renowned crabbiness. He's a freaking house! Of course he's going to be irritable. How would you like it, with the termites and the land tax and the having the dogs pee on your lawn?

GEMINI

Emotions run high as the coach spends an inordinate amount of time critiquing the singing of the team song. Stay out of it, Gemini. It won't do you any good to get involved. Wait until tempers have cooled before sneakily reigniting the argument with unflattering doodles you've made of your most short-tempered teammates. For best results, label them inaccurately, then use a black marker to draw a giant hole on a piece of butcher's paper before leaping through it into dimensions unknown.

CANCER

You're probably feeling more sensitive than usual today, Cancer, because of the retrograde movement of your batting partner after you called them through for an easy single only to have them not respond, leaving you stranded mid-pitch. Don't let your emotions overwhelm you. Focus instead on teaching your wicketkeeper how to start a fire using only the power of their mind. If the future of the Ashes doesn't lie in pyrokinesis, then we might as well give up now.

LEO

This isn't a good day to bowl a part-timer in the hope of buying an in-form batter's wicket, Leo. Ignore the temptation and instead work out your frustration by arguing with the umpires about the sphericality of the ball. Refuse to accept the evidence of the rings no matter how often the ball satisfies their purity tests. There are more dimensions than the pitiful three that our substandard physical senses can perceive. Demonstrate this to the umpires by fielding a cover point at right angles to reality.

VIRGO

Frustration with back-of-a-length bowling and a tight ring field could tempt you to release that energy by attempting a wild pull shot to a delivery that's not quite there. Try not to succumb, Virgo. Why not throw your energies instead into a creative pursuit, such as a song parody (Creativity Trigger: a ZZ Top-inspired knock-off: 'She's got leg-breaks! She knows how to use them') or a papier mâché model of Lord Ian Botham's junk.

LIBRA

What would you do, Libra, if you went to your kit only to discover that instead of it containing your bats, pads, gloves, jazz CDs, box and other vital equipment, it contained a sleeping vampire? The stump is right there, and with one swift driving motion, you could push it through the heart of this unholy nemesis of all that is proper in the world. Kudos to you. But then what if this 'vampire' turns out to instead simply be the team all-rounder, deeply embroiled in a game of hide-and-seek against your opening bowler? Think before you act.

SCORPIO

A hole in the cricket nets could lead to a training session taking far longer than it should, Scorpio. Especially when you discover that there is a dolphin trapped in the nets as well, flailing wildly as it fights against its inevitable demise. Try not to get frustrated at how a plague of overfishing has now spread far beyond the confines of the ocean and into local cricket training grounds. Focus instead on the smaller things that make life better. For example, tuna for lunch!

SAGITTARIUS

A mischievous team mate might get in your head, posing the question of how the Sri Lanka team of the mid-1990s and early 2000s got the name of 'Warnakulasuriya Patabendige Ushantha Joseph Chaminda Vaas' to properly scan when singing 'Happy Birthday' to the great left-arm seamer every 27th January. Try not to let their obvious ploy concern you. They probably just sang 'dear Chaminda' at the appropriate moment. Don't over-complicate things, Sagittarius. Have you tried yoga? Go for it!

CAPRICORN

A conflict between front foot and back foot strokeplay could arise today, Capricorn, as an inability to pick the length of a slower ball proves troubling. Try to think clearly about the nature of time, perhaps by conducting thought experiments such as what you would see if a torch was attached to Shoaib Akhtar as his run-up approached the speed of light. After all,

Einstein's footwork at the crease was always precise. I'm just saying.

AQUARIUS

This could be a challenging day, Aquarius. A bookmaker might attempt to blackmail you into giving them information on team selection or the plot of *Interstellar*. This will rightly enrage you, but it is important not to take it out on the insidious con artist when they call you with their vile demands. Remember: Don't shoot the messenger. Or, indeed, anybody. Who do you think you are?

PISCES

Vivid dreams are likely to cause you to wake up feeling angry, Pisces. Angry and chilled to the fabric of your very soul. This will disconcert your team mates, especially if your unrelenting screams of horror distract the rest of the slips cordon. But don't forget that a dream can only harm you if you let it, or if it contains Freddy Krueger. Space out the slips correctly and your panicked daytime sleep terror flailing will have less of an impact when a delivery takes the outside edge.

THE WICKET-KEEPER'S STATEMENT

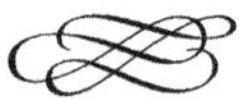

I've heard that a lot of the keyboard warrior wankers out there are challenging my integrity. Saying that I should have known that the catch didn't carry. But fuck me. I'm not the umpire. That's not my job. And people should be bloody well grateful for that. Because, you know that if I *was* the umpire, all the whingeing shitheads would lose their minds about that too. I can guaran-fucken-tee you that. Damned if I do, damned if I don't.

No, *my* first job is to get the ball into my gloves. And my second is to appeal for the catch. If the first is touch and go because, in some people's view, the ball's bounced, like, a millimetre - or maybe more, who can tell? - before it reached me, then all the *more* reason to go hard on the second part of the job. Get a good shout in. See if you can get the soft signal to go your way. Hope for some foreshortening on the camera angles. It's called profes-siona-fucken-lism. Look it up, dickheads.

Besides, it's not like I *forced* the third umpire to go with the onfield call. I'm not, like, running Xavier's School For Gifted fucken Youngsters out here. I don't have some kind of Professor

X bullshit mental control over him. I think we saw that when he ruled against the hit wicket appeal later in the session.

And just to clarify - since I seem to be getting an awful lot of fucken grief about that too - I was simply testing whether the bails were zing or not. I couldn't remember and rather than waste the time of the match officials or my captain by asking them, why not just flick one off with my gloves and see for myself? Question. Research. Hypothesis. Experiment. Results. Conclusion. That's how I did Science with Miss Farquar in Year 8. That's how I do science today. Or are we all suddenly against the scientific method? My deepest fucken apologies to everybody in this fucken theocracy we're now apparently living in. Apologies if I didn't notice, like, The Handmaid's Tale Stand here at the Gabba.

And, yes, because I know you're going to jump on me for this too, once the bails were on the ground, it just made sense to me to appeal for hit wicket. Am I supposed to keep track of every time I flick the bails off with my gloves? That's not my job. As far as I'm concerned, if I see the bails on the ground, I appeal for hit wicket. You can't train somebody out of doing that. Or if you can, they're a piss-poor excuse for a wicketkeeper.

Now, you're probably going to ask if, after that incident, I regret calling the batsman a 'lucky fucken duke of limbs who should fuck off back to the dressing room for some fussock-love.'

And the answer is, I don't. I'm not in charge of the stump microphone. That's not my job. Do I look like a sound engineer? Am I Ben fucken Burtt all of a sudden?

No, of *course* I have a chat with the batsman while they're at the crease. And before any of you PC dickheads come at me - I'm not going to call him a 'batter'. I'm not one of those enlightened 'look at me, I'm tolerant of everybody who wants to play the game' type of poseurs, always changing terminology to be 'inclusive' or 'respectful'. It's not my job to be tolerant or considerate of other people's feelings. It's my job to keep wicket.

Not that I have anything against women playing. Women playing cricket is great. They're great. Good on them. I just don't see why I should be saying 'batters' when I can be saying 'batsman'. It's a man with a bat in his hand - he's either a batsman, or a Batman, and I don't see no Christian fucken Bale or underrated Val Kilmer out there, if you get my drift. And the smart-arses who say 'you don't say fieldsman or bowlsman, do you?' Well, maybe I will. Don't tell me what I can't do or say. I'm a wicket-keeper. My whole job is to say shit that will upset people. Anything to give the bowlsman a better chance to take a wicket.

Fuck me, it's bad enough we've been told to let 'Chinaman' go, just because it upsets people who consider it a racial slur. When all it ever was was a way of describing left-arm wrist spin, that *just happens* to sound like a racial slur. Sure, it upsets many people, but it doesn't upset me, and yet I'm the one who is supposed to change how I talk about the game? Maybe we can find a compromise - bit of give and take, meet in the middle - and call them a left-arm wrist spinsman? If that's okay with The Woke Police?

I don't understand why we can't just use the same terminology we've always used. This change in the fucken lexicon does me head in. It's not my job to worry about women or minorities. It's my job to keep wicket.

And yes, before you ask, I *am* disappointed with the three dropped catches and the missed stumpings. And, of course, in an ideal world, I'd prefer to have conceded a couple of dozen fewer byes. But that's cricket for you. Tough game.

EXCERPT FROM 'CRICKET MAGIC FOR CRICKET TRAGICS' BY GLENN AND MULLER

Cricket magicians Glenn (McGrath) and (Scott) Muller are famous around the world for their award-winning shows that combine cricket magic with bawdy comedy. Here's an excerpt from their slim but influential introduction to the art of cricketing magic, Cricket Magic for Cricket Tragics

Deceived In Flight

Now that you've mastered some of the more basic tricks - Steve Waugh's never-ending red rag, the linked ball-testing rings, palming the coin toss, etc. - it's time to progress to a more complicated trick. We call it 'Deceived In Flight'.

As with all cricket magic, the success of this trick depends on preparation, misdirection and countless hours of practice. But the reward for that effort is an illusion sure to amaze batters and spectators alike, like a Rishabh Pant innings or an over from Marnus Labuschagne.

Follow these simple steps and you'll soon master 'Deceived In Flight'.

1. Move to the top of your mark, being sure to maintain your patter. (See *Appendix A: Making The Patter Play* for detailed guidelines on how to tailor your patter to your own personality, whether that's keeping it light and fun or calling the batter a 'complete fuck**t c**t')

2. Grip the ball with the seam between index and middle finger. Your thumb should be under the ball and your wrist cocked. The grip is the key to this trick, so practise using a mirror (borrow one from Marcus Stoinis if necessary) to ensure you get it right.

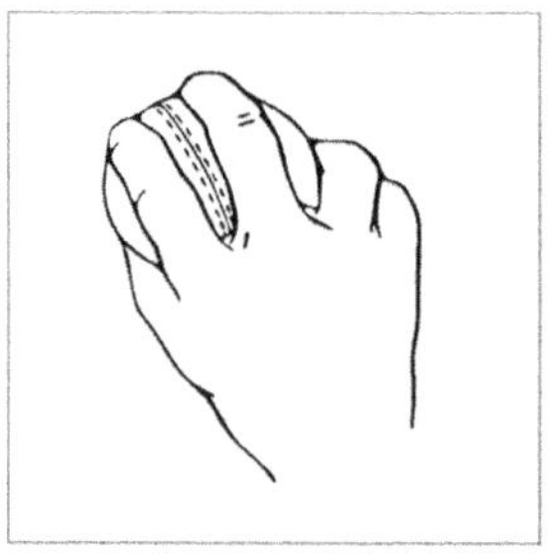

Grip at the top of your mark

3. Now you will commence your run-up. It's often good cricket magic technique here to put the batter at ease by assuring them that all you have in your hand is a cricket ball. Demonstrate, if necessary, that you have nothing up your sleeves by rolling them up above your elbow. This will also help reassure the umpire that you are not a chucker.

4. As you run in, maintain eye contact with the batter. At some point they will look down, tapping their bat on the ground as they wait for your arrival at the crease. If they are Steve Smith, they may fidget, suddenly step across their crease or begin needlessly shadow-batting. Do not be distracted. Focus on their eyes. The instant they look away is your opportunity to use

your honed sleight of hand skills. You may only have a split-second in which to act, so again, this is where your hours of rehearsal pay off.

5. Once the batter is looking away from you, simply use your thumb to crack the shell of the cricket ball, which as you've probably realised by now is not, in fact, a cricket ball but instead a dove egg that you carefully painted earlier so that it *looked like* a cricket ball. This is the same dove egg that you took from your pocket after palming the cricket ball during your patter in Step 1.

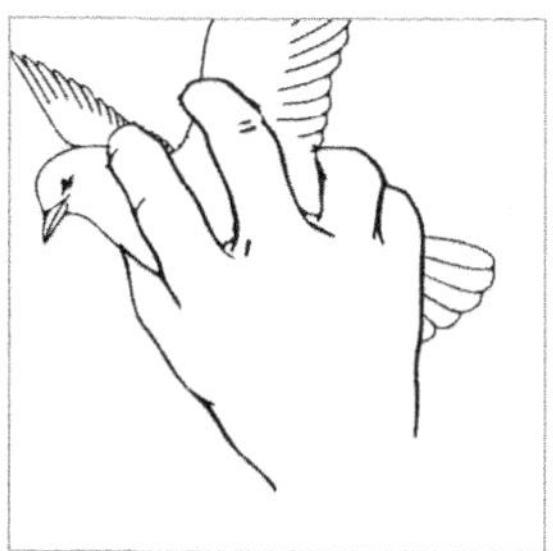

Grip just prior to release

6. Continue to tear open the egg shell as you begin your delivery stride. By the time you release the ball, the shell should be sufficiently broken that the dove inside can fly out and away, amazing everybody in attendance. (Can newly hatched doves fly? There's only one way to find out.)

And that's the Deceived In Flight illusion. As always with cricket magic, it's easy once you know how.

Next: Sawing the umpire in half

NO THRILLING CONCLUSION TO A MATCH HAS EVER BEEN LEGITIMATE

You may think you've enjoyed some thrilling conclusions to cricket matches. You may have revelled in the drama, the tension, the roar of the crowd.

Sad, then, to think that your enjoyment of those matches was wrong. Because no thrilling conclusion to a match has ever been legitimate. This, I'm afraid, is the cold, harsh truth.

Let's go through some famous examples.

2ND TEST, 2005 ASHES - ENGLAND WIN BY 2 RUNS

It's the moment that saved arguably the greatest Test series ever played. The 2005 Ashes was an ebbing, flowing thrill-ride, riding in with the most flowing thrills and thrilling us with the most ebbing ride in Birmingham in the second Test.

It was a Test that England dominated for most of the match. Until somehow, improbably, a Shane-Warne-led counterattack saw Australia on the brink of stealing the match from them.

Sixteen months later, we'd see that if a Shane Warne-led counterattack against a dominant England side was allowed to blossom into a victory then it led inexorably to a whitewashed series.

For the good of the series, then, Steve Harmison had Michael Kasprowicz caught behind with Australia still 3 runs shy of a win.

Except, of course, that Kasprowicz's hand was off the bat and so the catch shouldn't have been given.

3RD TEST, 2019 ASHES - ENGLAND WIN BY 1 WICKET

It was one of the greatest knocks of all time from a certified Impossible Person in Ben Stokes. From the ignominy of 67 all out, Stokes led England's resurgence, taking 3/56 from 24.2 overs (50% more than any other bowler in the England attack that innings) to keep the fourth innings target to something that was merely infinitesimally unlikely rather than impossible.

And then, with 73 runs still needed, and number 11 Jack Leach joining him, Stokes combined power hitting, T20 unorthodoxy and strike manipulation to bedevil the Australian bowlers and captain, before finally crashing the ball for four for a remarkable win. The Headingley crowd roared.

A shame, then, that DRS replays confirm that he should have been given out LBW to Nathan Lyon the over before.

ODI WORLD CUP FINAL 2019, SCORES TIED, ENGLAND WIN ON BOUNDARY COUNTBACK

Headingley was not the only scene of Stokes' magic-wielding that 2019 summer. During the World Cup final, he'd found himself in a similarly precarious position in a run chase against New Zealand.

Once again, he was the rock holding the chase together. If such a concept is possible. A rock with hands? Or magnets perhaps? Who can say.

Perhaps it's more accurate, metaphorically, to say that Stokes was an astronaut in a spacesuit in a hurricane, trying to maintain a grip. Except, that doesn't work either. A hurricane in the vacuum of space? How does that work?

Look, the point is that England were screwed. Just as they were at Headingley. Except more so, because this time they had the further constraint of a limited number of balls in which to get the runs.

And yet Stokes got them close.

With three balls remaining, England had two wickets in hand and needed nine runs to win. Stokes was on strike. He thwacked Trent Boult to deep midwicket and scurried back for a second to retain the strike. As a result of his dive, the ball hit his outstretched bat and raced away for four overthrows. Two became six, with two more singles (and run outs) off the last two balls ensuring a tie and a super over that would earn England the World Cup.

Except, of course, as many cricket Laws-wielders have poindextered out by now, the overthrows that ultimately levelled the match should have only resulted in five runs, not six. No tie. No Super Over. No England World Cup win.

ODI WORLD CUP SECOND SEMI-FINAL 1999, SCORES TIED, AUSTRALIA ADVANCE ON SUPERIOR NET RUN RATE

But it's not just England wins (or ties that count as wins) that are illegitimate. Twenty years earlier, Australia and South Africa played out a heart-stopping semi-final that ended with both teams level on 213 all out.

The final moments of the match will live forever in infamy. With scores level and four balls remaining, player of the tournament Lance Klusener clubbed the ball back past bowler Damien Fleming to Mark Waugh fielding at mid-off. Klusener took off for the single, only to discover non-striker Allan Donald more concerned with regaining his ground.

By the time Klusener had completed his run, Donald had yet to begin. He belatedly attempted to do so, *sans* bat for some reason, only for the unsportsmanlike Fleming to underarm the ball to Adam Gilchrist to complete the run out.

Technically, Fleming's rolling of the ball was legal, but it was a clear violation of the spirit of the game. Australia should have known better after the similarly infamous underarm incident against New Zealand almost two decades earlier.

But no. The ugly Aussies will do anything to win (or, in this case, tie), no matter how shameful. Even Gilchrist knew, shaking his head as Fleming prepared to roll it. And the ordinarily parochial Bill Lawry on commentary was similarly disappointed by the men in yellow, shouting 'I cannot believe it!'

1ST TEST, SOUTH AFRICA V SRI LANKA 2018/19

This forgotten twin of Stokes' Headingley heroics saw Kusal Perera, the man affectionately known as KP, score 153 not out.

He partnered Vishwa Fernando for over an hour in an unbeaten 78 run partnership to snatch a one wicket win from South Africa, who had earlier reduced Sri Lanka to 110/5 in pursuit of the 304 they needed for victory.

Fending off Dale Steyn and Kagiso Rabada, Perera's batting heroics became instantly the stuff of legend, brought down only marginally because he carelessly failed to showcase the knock while playing in an Ashes series. Nevertheless, it was an innings that merits several thousand pages of analysis, an epic of uncomplicated heroics. A history, a love poem and a chronicle, half a million words or more, all of them true.

Which is why it's such a shame that Perera's innings can be statistically proven to have broken the laws of probability. In this modern day and age, it's simply not on for this kind of wishful, unscientific innings. Probability theory is a legitimate branch of mathematics. You can't just abandon it because you'd really like to win a Test match, Kusal.

OTHERS

It's not just those five innings of course. Every close finish you can think of has been tainted by illegitimacy.

Some more examples:

- Michael Clarke's three wickets in an over to beat India at the SCG in 2007/8? Ruined by the bowler wielding distracting blond tips.
- Ian Botham dismissing Jeff Thomson in 1982/83 to give England a 3 run win? Pretty unfair, don't you think, to have people catching dropped chances, as Geoff Miller did when Chris Tavare spilt the edge to slip. Catching a

drop fundamentally negates the entire *concept* of a drop. Disappointing England would stoop to such levels.

- Both tied Tests? Riddled with numerous errors of addition. When accountants audited the scorecards in later years, they discovered that the Gabba Tied Test should, in fact, have been a 131 run win to the West Indies. Really sloppy home team scoring.

I could go on but I think the point has been made. If you enjoyed these or any other close finishes to a cricket match, you were wrong to do so.

FIVE TIE-BREAKERS

AN IDEA FOR FIXING CRICKET MATCHES

PROBLEM WITH CURRENT LAW

Too much time is wasted in the modern game determining if a lofted shot into the outfield has gone a smidgen over the boundary rope for six or landed just inside it for four. This is particularly problematic when it seems to land almost on the half-volley of the rope. A third umpire can rock and roll the replay back and forth multiple times in slow motion before ultimately shrugging and resorting to their best guess about where the ball first landed.

PROPOSED SOLUTION

If it takes more than one replay to determine if a shot is a four or a six it should be called a five and that's the end of it.

IMPLEMENTATION

Whenever it's not immediately clear whether a particular shot has fallen inside the rope, the short-sighted and/or dimwitted onfield umpire will radio their all-seeing television counterpart for clarification, much like they currently do. But there will be no mucking about from the thirdie. A single replay will be viewed and immediately afterward they'll send back a decision for either four, six or five runs.

PROS

- Can save up to fifteen to thirty seconds over an entire T20 international or ODI. This time can be used for an extra television advertisement, making cricket a more financially viable sport
- If the occasions when the third umpire sends back a five are genuinely 50-50 propositions then, on average over time, players will end up with the same overall runs as they would otherwise have scored had the third umpire taken the time and effort to determine precisely the nature of the boundary. So, again, why waste everybody's time? Life is precious, man
- If teams are truly desperate to save or score the extra run, they can use a review to force the third umpire to have a proper look at it. Without that extra willingness to risk a review from the captain, however, the umpire must resist the urge for precision and instead go with their first look of 'yep, that's a six', 'nah, that's a four' or 'fucked if I know, let's call it five'

CONS

- Makes fives less special - no longer can we be reasonably confident that there has been a comical overthrow to help the scoring along. Countering this, it will make overthrow fives that much more relatable.

"Oh look," fans will be able to say, as the wild ping from the idiot at cover point sails past the stumps and flies towards the boundary. "It's as if the batter hit a ball that landed incredibly close to a rope. Isn't that adorable."

- The increase in fives will require an extra column in most cricket statistics databases. This could be ameliorated, however, by attributing fives to existing four and six columns based on what numbered match the batter is playing. For example, if it's an odd-numbered match (eg, their first, third, seventh, one-hundred and ninth, etc), all fives are added to the player's tally of fours. If it's an even-numbered match, the fives are added to their tally of sixes. Again, over time, this will probabilistically even out. (And, to be clear, they will get five added to their runs tally - we're just talking about the stats for numbers of boundaries here.)
- *However*, if the above approach for attributing fives to existing boundary database fields is applied, it is technically possible for a batter to have five career runs but credited as having scored a six. (Or any multiple thereof.) Any player who manages this should be awarded a special Statistical Outlier Cap from the ICC which they will be permitted to wear throughout their career

FURTHER NOTES

The signal for a five scored in this manner will, much like the runs themselves, be an interpolation of the signals for a four and a six. The umpire will raise both hands above their heads and sway them back and forth like a boomer listening to Paul McCartney sing 'Hey Jude'.

SIR ALASTAIR COOK V SIR DONALD BRADMAN

Many people like to go on and on about Sir Donald Bradman. Greatest batter ever. Freakish talent. Unsurpassable career. Blah, blah, blah.

But was the Don really all, as the kids like to say, that?

I put it to you that he was not. Let's compare him to a randomly chosen cricketer of a more modern era - say, fellow knight Sir Alastair Cook.

Some might say that Cook was just an enduring Test opener for England, nurdling and nudging his way up the record books, one clip off the hip at a time, sometimes tossing coins in a blazer before the game begun, sometimes not.

And yet, a detailed statistical breakdown of Cook's career reveals that Cook was much more than that. By any reasonable analysis, he's a better Test cricketer than Bradman.

Let's break it down.

BATTING AVERAGE

Bradman has the initial advantage here, averaging 99.94 to Cook's 45.35. So let's give that one to The Don, despite the fact he never had to face Stuart Clark in his prime.

BRADMAN: 1
COOK: 0

TOTAL TEST RUNS

Cook scored 12,472 runs in his Test career, compared to Bradman's mere 6,996. If Bradman has an average twice as good as Cook's, Cook's run tally is almost as proportionally dominant. And by my reckoning, that just about evens things up.

BRADMAN: 1
COOK: 1

HIGHEST SCORE

The Don made 334 runs at his peak, whereas Cook's top score was 294. It's close, but I suppose technically we have to give the points to Bradman, even though 40 runs is barely anything when you think about it.

BRADMAN: 2
COOK: 1

NUMBER OF CENTURIES

While Bradman tallied 29 centuries in his Test career, Cook made his way out of the nervous twenties and took his total number of tons to 33. So points to the mentally tough Cook here.

BRADMAN: 2
COOK: 2

At the end of this initial analysis, we're even on batting. Let's move to bowling to break the tie.

NUMBER OF WICKETS

Bradman took two wickets in his Test career. Cook just the one. Advantage Bradman. I guess.

BRADMAN: 3
COOK: 2

BOWLING AVERAGE

Cook's bowling average is 6.00, one of the very best of all time. In comparison, Bradman's bowling average is a mediocre 36.00. Big advantage to Cook here.

BRADMAN: 3
COOK: 3

Amazingly, we still can't separate the pair even after we take bowling into consideration. Let's move on to fielding.

CATCHES

Bradman took 32 catches in his career, an impressive effort for a man so old he's technically dead. But Cook covers him easily, plucking 175 deliveries out of the air to send idiot batters on their way.

BRADMAN: 3
COOK: 4

STUMPINGS

Bradman did not complete a single stumping in his career. And while Cook didn't manage one either, the fact remains that Cook could come out of retirement at any moment, take the gloves and pull ahead still further. Which gives him an undeniable edge.

BRADMAN: 3
COOK: 5

CAPTAINCY

Let's round out the analysis by looking at the captaincy of both players. Bradman captained Australia to victory on just 15 occasions, a truly paltry amount compared to the quality leadership of Cook, who was triumphant an amazing 24 times. Advantage Alastair, yet again.

BRADMAN: 3
COOK: 6

There we have it. A robust and fair analysis of these two cricketers leaves us in no doubt. Sir Alastair Cook, a randomly chosen knighted cricketer, is *twice* as good as Sir Donald Bradman, who, in retrospect, should probably have his knighthood posthumously stripped from him. So let's chill it with all the hype, huh?

CRYPTIC CROSSWORD 3

BOWLING

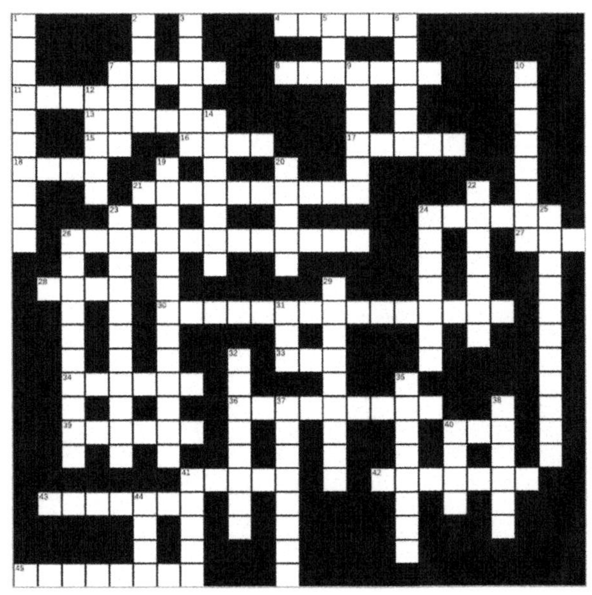

Across

4 Bowled early, yet others recognised knock ended disastrously (6)

7 I'm sad, it seems, that I have the golden touch? (5)

8 A remarkable one-legged leap makes one sit up (4,3)

11 The captain defeated the final bowler (6)

13 Max didn't hang around (6)

15 Batting will start, no need to ask (2)

16 Recklessly dare to predict which way it'll spin (4)

17 Drop a catch to help the bowler (5)

18 Spin will ultimately defeat the holder of the Ashes (4)

21 A gift that's not totally lovely, perhaps (4-6)

24 & 1D A great delivery, but one that brings up a ton (4,2,3,7)

26 Beefy was bored by - loathed, in retrospect - run-of-the-mill bowling (5,8)

27 A ball that's easy to hit? Sounds irrational (3)

28 Stuart would blow his top bowling on this (4)

30 Bowling angle for a Bodyline field placement (6,3,6)

33 Not a good score? You've got that backwards (3)

34 Some would ban a nation that swings it like this (6)

36 Ball may require a knee surgeon (3,6)

39 The best place to bowl, by some distance... (6)

40 Dead ball? You'll have to spin it hard (3)

41 Lopes in casually to exploit the Lord's pitch (5)

42 Impossible ball to play - a terminal batting eraser (7)

43 Delivery is a badly worn shooter! (7)

45 Time to get back to work turning it away from left-handers (3,5)

Down

1 See 24A

2 Spin it back, around the wicket, initially right, then left (5)

3 Dangerous ball from smiling bowler (6)

5 Work the single (3)

6 Bowl this one on a road. So much spin (6)

7 Typical persona of a fast bowler (4)

9 A ball that makes a batter go forward, then go back, then left dizzy in the end (6)

10 Easily hit, with plenty of flight around a turning ball (8)

12 Movement through the air like it has some kind of wings (5)

14 I hear he's a gun umpire (7)

19 Go fetch a blank, new pitch (short, but not too short) (4,2,1,6)

20 Casually ogle clips of very handy coverage (5)

22 Face this one with a bit of a stiff lip, perhaps (7)

23 Delay the finish by bowling defensively (4,2,2,3)

24 Tough to keep out nuisance delivery (7)

25 Acting fresh in some way because they didn't open the bowling (5,6)

26 Rebowls all wild deliveries (and those that are tamer) (6,4)

29 It's kind of chic, minus the bouncers (4,5)

31 Party time for the batter? No (3)

32 A ball that creates no trouble or panic, but carries some kind of toll (4,4)

35 A difficult ball to bowl, or even to begin the run up? (3,5)

37 A cap for the debutant on a tricky pitch (5,3)

38 A quiet, suffering plea. Or is it? (6)

40 Start ripping in bouncers, smashing tender body parts (4)

41 The edge is off to cover point (5)

44 Out? Not out? Recalled and put back in, for example (4)

BRADMAN AVERAGE JOKES

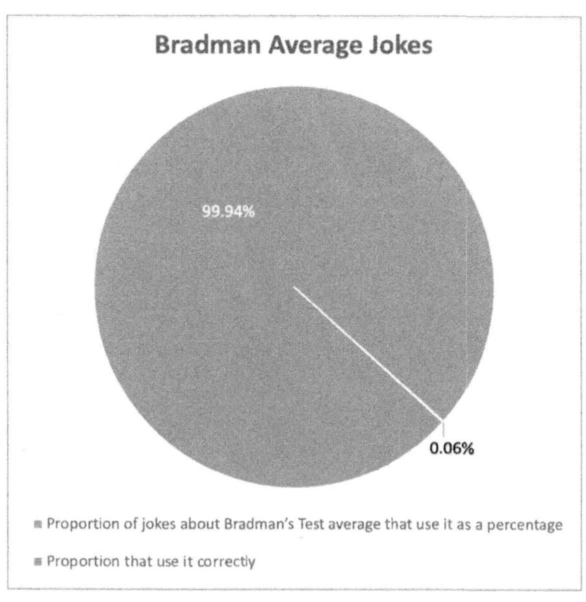

THE MYSTERY OF THE MISSING MITCH MARSH

A TRAGIC DETECTIVE MYSTERY

28 runs were needed from 17 balls when Security barged into our row. There were two of them, of widely varying degrees of squatness.

The detective looked up, fury and conjunctivitis in his eyes, as the two guards shoved their way towards him.

“What the fu—” he began, before they reached past him to the woman in the green sun dress, who had been sitting beside us all day.

She looked up in surprise as the more squat security guard began to talk to her. The detective craned his head around the less squat guard in an attempt to gain an unhindered view of the action.

Out in the middle, Chris Rogers turned a ball off his hip. He scampered hard between the wickets, returning for a second run that, while not technically *necessitating* a dive, was in no way rejecting such an option. The sellout crowd, boosted by heavy ticket sales from chrisrogersEZcrickettickets.com cheered the effort.

26 runs from 16 balls required.

As Rogers picked himself up and dusted off, the woman protested.

"You've got the wrong person," she said.

"I don't think so, Miss," said the less squat security guard.

"Sit down!!" yelled the dunderwhelps behind us, who'd spent much of the run chase failing to start a Mexican wave, with their drunken, bellowed countdowns invariably initiating instead foul-mouthed epithets, that were thrust at all their non-wave-initiating neighbours.

The guards predictably ignored their abuse. Much as they'd earlier ignored their tendency to spill beer all over the people they were trying to step past, as well as their loud, unschooled discussions in which they'd consistently misinterpreted the nuances of the LBW Law.

The woman, however, was having no such luck in shaking off the guards' attention.

"I'm not going anywhere with you," she said.

The guards looked back to the end of the row from which they'd emerged. A goateed fusspot now stood there, glowering furiously. He pointed and nodded. "That's definitely her," he said.

The guards grabbed the woman. She wrenched her arm away from their grasp.

"Let go of me," she said, as the detective shifted angles to look instead at the big screen.

The next ball whistled past the outside edge of Rogers' bat. The crowd groaned at the dot. The groans in our vicinity then became boos as the woman was dragged out of her seat. The clodpates behind us started a chant, before aborting it almost immediately amid great confusion as to its precise phrasing.

26 runs from 15 balls required.

"Leave me alone, you pigs," said the woman.

With a world-weary sigh, the detective placed his final beer of the evening beneath his seat and leant over.

"What's going on?" he said.

"This woman stole a Mitch Marsh action figure from the gift shop," said the squat one.

"I most certainly did not."

"The GSCF says you did - he's positively identified you."

"GSCF?" I whispered to the detective.

"Gift Shop Customer Facilitator," the detective replied. He turned back to the woman. "You *did* just return to your seat," he pointed out.

"I left to go to the bathroom," she said.

"With three overs remaining?" said the detective.

"Do *you* want to try to get into the women's bathrooms after the match?" she shot back, presumably rhetorically. Whatever unspoken camaraderie had been built over the last seven hours of sitting beside one another was now shattered. "And what business of it is yours anyway?" she added.

The detective paused the conversation with a raising of his hand. This time, Rogers played a late cut that beat the third man fielder. A critical boundary that met with much roaring. He called for a change of gloves. The opener had anchored the entire run chase with a sensible, measured innings and now seemed determined to bring it home.

22 runs from 14 balls required.

The detective applauded, then turned back to the guards, where he signalled for the resumption of the conversation with his next question.

"What, exactly, is this woman accused of?"

"The GSCF saw a brunette woman in a plain green dress grab the action figure and disappear from the shop," said the squat guard.

I watched as the detective ran his gaze over her. Plain green dress. Brunette. Woman. That part of the story checked out, as it had throughout the entire day's play.

"She then fled from the store, and disappeared up this bay," continued the guard. "The GSCF was too busy getting the AGSCF to take over the cash register to follow immediately, but as soon as he was able to do so, he notified us. Fortunately for us, she's the only brunette woman in a plain green dress here."

I looked around the bay. There were other women, of course. Many of them brunette. But these others were all wearing shorts and tank tops. Or jeans and baby tees. Or dresses, but either patterned or of different colours.

The squat guard glanced back at the GSCF at the edge of the row and he nodded again vigorously.

"Then he's an idiot," said the woman. "You can search me if you like."

"That's exactly what we plan to do," said the less squat guard. "Now come on."

The next ball to Rogers was driven through the covers. It beat the fielder sprinting around from deep point to reach the boundary. The crowd bellowed raucous approval at this outcome.

18 runs from 13 balls required.

"Don't you have CCTV?" asked the detective. "Surely that would sort this out."

"We will be referring to that as well," said the squat guard.

"I'm not missing the end of this match," said the woman.

"Can't you wait?" asked the detective. "She's been here from the first ball. It'd be cruel to deny her the last two overs."

The squat guard looked at the scoreboard and pondered the prospect of instigating a modicum of common sense.

On the field, the bowler signalled his intention to come around the wicket.

The less squat guard beckoned the GSCF over.

"Down in front!!" yelled the hooligans again, as the GSCF squeezed down our row. It was a request that would have merited more consideration had they at any point during the previous 98 overs of play shown more than a passing interest in the on-field action.

"Can we wait until the end of the match?" the squat guard asked of the GSCF.

"How long to go?" he replied.

"2.1 overs," said the less squat guard, pointing to the appropriate subsection of the digital scoreboard.

"Oh, definitely not then," said the GSCF. "I have to get back *now*. I've got six crates of Lego Chris Rogers action sets on an Express Delivery from the warehouse for the after-match rush." He let the thought trail away, before his eyes widened at the bowlers' figures. "Ravi Bopara 3/18?? Looks like I need to get some Boptimus Prime figures unpacked too." He pulled out his mobile phone and began tapping furiously.

The last ball of the over was delivered. It was full and angled in at leg stump. The ball beat Rogers' hurried bat and crashed into his pad before deflecting into the wicket, sending the bails crashing to the ground.

A gasp of deflation echoed around the stadium.

18 runs from 12 balls required. But now without the set batter.

"Right," said the less squat guard. "Seriously. Let's go."

The two guards grabbed an arm each of the woman and urged her out of her seat.

"I can't believe this," said the woman. "I'm going to demand a full refund, you know."

"Enough of your lies," said the GSCF. "I know for certain you're the shoplifter."

"And I know for certain she isn't," said the detective.

The detective has solved the mystery of the shoplifted Mitch Marsh action figure. Have you??

"HOW WOULD YOU KNOW WHAT I SAW?" ASKED THE GSCF.

"Tell me how many runs Chris Rogers scored," the detective asked. He gestured to the scoreboard.

There was a long pause. "I don't know," admitted the GSCF eventually.

"He can't see?" said the woman.

"Oh, he can see," said the detective. "Just a moment ago, he read the England bowling figures perfectly well. But they're displayed in a completely different combination of colours." The detective smiled. "A combination more sensitive to the challenges faced by colour-blind individuals such as Chris Rogers. Or, indeed, our GSCF here."

"You're colour-blind?" asked the squat security guard of the GSCF.

"Let me guess," continued the detective to the guards. "It was you two who determined that this woman seated beside me was the only one in this bay in a plain green dress, right?"

"Correct."

He pointed to a woman five rows ahead and several seats over. "What about her?"

"Well, she's wearing a heavily patterned green dress," said the less squat guard, as if the detective were an idiot.

The detective turned to the GSCF.

"Is that what you see?"

"I don't see any pattern," he admitted.

"Just as I suspected," said the detective. He turned to the guards. "Go search *her* bag. She'll have the shoplifted Mitch Marsh action figure."

And, of course, she did, along with a Peter Taylor Pogo Stick, a copy of Andy Bichel's *To Be The Twelfth* and a tube of George Bailey toothpaste.

Another injustice averted and cricketing crime spree undone, thanks to the detective's amazing deductive prowess! Stay tuned for further baffling mysteries that can only be solved by the sleuth of slower balls, the gumshoe of googlies, the investigator of inside edges: the Tragic Detective.

THIS YEAR'S WINNERS AT CRICKETTECH - THE LEADING CRICKET TECHNOLOGY CONFERENCE

OUTSTANDING INNOVATION IN PLAYER TECHNOLOGY - UMPIRETRUST™ CLASSIC GLOVE AND BAT COMBO

Remember the days before Snicko and Hot Spot (and their generic brand equivalents)? The glory days of cricket when a batter could feather one behind and get away with it should they be sufficiently stone-faced not to betray their errant touch on the ball, and brave enough to stare the umpire down despite the fevered braying of the bowler and slips cordon?

Those days are back! Turn that 'out' into 'the benefit of the doubt' with UmpireTrust™'s Classic Glove and Bat Combo.

Once paired, the noise-cancelling chip in the thumb of the gloves will detect a ball striking the edge of the bat. UmpireTrust™'s patented Play'n'Miss AI will then generate an inverted sound wave of the precise frequency necessary to negate the sound of the nick.

From there, the relative speeds of sound and light and close proximity of the gloves to the edge of the bat combine to get the job done. The absence of sound waves not only makes the feathered chance inaudible to human ears but also to any technology the third umpire may wish to deploy.

Plus, UmpireTrust™'s famous CoolEdge bat technology is now 34% faster! Any edge on the bat is detected and instantly cooled - in more than 80% of cases, *in between* frames of any Hot Spot (or Hot Spot-like) technology.

Worried that the AI might kick in and deny you salvation from an edge onto your pads in an LBW shout? Worry no longer. Detailed analysis of tens of thousands of such edges means that UmpireTrust™'s world-famous Play'n'Miss AI is now capable of entering Inside Edge Mode.

Once in Inside Edge Mode, sophisticated heuristics and groundbreaking new WarmEdge technology will combine to provide the evidence most likely to keep you at the crease, based on the UmpireTrust™ algorithm's determination of whether the inside edge has flown through to the keeper or gone on to thump the pads.

Fight technology with technology.

UmpireTrust™ Classic Glove and Bat Combo - All's fair in glove and bats

OUTSTANDING INNOVATION IN OFFICIATING TECHNOLOGY - TELL-ALL TELEPATHY HELMETS (AND ASSOCIATED GIZMOTIVE DEVICE)

Is that a dead ball or a leg bye? A valid LBW shout or not?

Too often, cricket decisions rely on umpires inferring the *intent* of the batter and whether they were playing a genuine shot.

It is an unreasonable requirement. Umpires are not telepaths or philosophers or gods.

Or, at least, they weren't.

Thanks to modern technology, it is now possible for umpires to *truly* understand the motivations of the batters, thanks to the Tell-All Telepathic Helmet.

Trained on 30,000 net-hours of Jedi leaves to reverse sweeps and everything in between, the Tell-All Telepathic Helmet uses EEG technology to measure electrical activity in the brain via small electrodes on the inside of the helmet. From there, the signals are transmitted to the umpire's pocket-sized Gizmotive Device, which uses neural network technology to convert those signals into a simple 'playing a shot' or 'not playing a shot' decision.

Say goodbye to unearned leg byes. Know the line on whether it matters that batters were struck outside the line.

Tell-All Telepathic Helmets - it's mind over batter.

HONOURABLE MENTIONS

ZING BOUNDARIES

ZingCorp is back with yet another stunning new Zing breakthrough.

Not content with brightening up every bowled dismissal, stumping and run out with the classic Zing Bails, ZingCorp has turned its flashing red eye to the boundary.

Slo-mo replays of diving fielders desperately trying to prevent fours are a thing of the past with Zing Boundaries.

Triggered by either an electromagnetically lacquered ball passing over it (lacquer available in red, white *and* pink), or a pulse transmitted through the fielder's body whenever they are in contact with both the ball and the rope, Zing Boundaries provide instant four feedback.

Flashy fours deserve flashing fours.

ZingCorp, you've done it again!

THE THESAURUS BOX

Is there anything more degrading than being hit in the one-eyed trouser snake? Of course there is - listening to commentators stifle their sniggering as they stumble for an appropriate euphemism for the blow to your love truncheon.

If you're writhing on the ground, having copped one in the pork-sword, the last thing you want to know is that the commentators are talking about 'nether regions' and 'groin areas'.

The Thesaurus Box dissuades such tiresome jocular coyness. Programmed with over 8000 synonyms for your penis, a devastating blow to the box fires off its final words - a loudly broadcast, randomly chosen, moniker for your Master John Goodfellow.

Once the word is out, it becomes virtually impossible for the commentators to refer to your custard launcher by anything other than the name your Thesaurus Box has bestowed upon it.

If you must be struck in the sausage sceptre, at least have the consolation that Mike Atherton may be forced to refer to it as your 'hairy canary'.

Also available - The Thesaurus Box, Vajayjay Edition

THE SLEDGE

A comedy writer knocks on the door of Tim Paine's office, a few weeks prior to the 2021/22 Ashes.

COMEDY WRITER
You wanted to see me?

TIM PAINE
Yes, yes. Come in, come in, comedy writer who may be a man *or* a woman. All very inclusive here.

COMEDY WRITER
(confused)
I'm sorry?

TIM PAINE
(ignoring them)
I want to talk to you about the latest sledge you've written for me. Take a seat.

The comedy writer does so.

TIM PAINE
(continuing)
Now, as you know, I employed you a couple of months ago to 'punch up' my material. After all, if the Barmy Army is going to be making jokes about Joe Root being a better batter than me, I need better comebacks than 'haw, well at least I'm a better batter than *you*'. So I've hired you to write me some fresh sledges that will really get people taking notice of me and saying 'that Tim Paine, he's still got it'. (Unless, of course, I'm forced to resign in disgrace before the Ashes even begins.)

COMEDY WRITER
That was terribly expository, wasn't it?

TIM PAINE
Yes, it was. And it's exactly the kind of poor writing I want to expunge from my repertoire.

COMEDY WRITER
Well, that's what I'm here for.

TIM PAINE
It is indeed.
(he pulls out a piece of paper from his desk drawer)
Now, about this most recent sledge you've written...

COMEDY WRITER
It's good, isn't it?

TIM PAINE
Well, let's talk about that.

COMEDY WRITER
You don't like it?

TIM PAINE

(reading from the piece of paper)

'Hey, fellas. This guy's got more unexpected shots than an Alec Baldwin movie set'.

COMEDY WRITER

It refers to that accidental shooting on the set of the movie *Rust*. It's edgy.

TIM PAINE

Yes, I get the reference. But...

COMEDY WRITER

I thought you could use it sarcastically. Like if a hopeless duffer with the bat comes in - say a Jimmy Anderson or a Zak Crawley - and goes for a reverse sweep that he misses and gets hit in the grill. Then you pull out the sledge, but with a sarcastic tone - like, he *has* unexpected shots but the subtext is they're pretty terrible.

TIM PAINE

No, no. I understand when and how I'd theoretically use the sledge. That's not the problem.

COMEDY WRITER

Because it's wordplay. When you say 'shot' in cricket, you mean a stroke that the batsman—

TIM PAINE

(hurriedly)

Batter

COMEDY WRITER

—batter is playing. But the 'shot' on the set of *Rust* was a loaded gun going off in the face of a member of the crew.

TIM PAINE

Yes, I understand the wordplay. But that's kind of the problem. I mean, a woman died in that accident. It was a tragedy.

COMEDY WRITER

Sure.

TIM PAINE

Somebody will almost certainly go to jail for the incident. I'm not sure I want to be seen as the Australian captain making fun of that.

COMEDY WRITER

(frowning in confusion)

But I thought you hired me to generate edgier material for you.

TIM PAINE

Well, this one might be a bit *too* edgy. Can't you come up with slightly less controversial edgy material?

COMEDY WRITER

(sighing)

I could try.

(beat)

What about something to do with 'shots' as in vaccinations, which is still a hot button issue here in late 2021? I could brainstorm some ideas on that. The opposite take: 'This guy's got *fewer* shots than an anti-vaxxer'.

TIM PAINE
(unconvinced)
Again, I don't really want to be taking any kind of public stance on matters of importance. I just want some light, fun comedy. Like, y'know, the babysitting bit.

COMEDY WRITER
But edgier?

TIM PAINE
Exactly.

COMEDY WRITER
(after a moment's thought)
What about if somebody drops an easy catch? 'This guy's messed up more sitters than Michael Myers'?

TIM PAINE
(confused)
The *Austin Powers* guy?

COMEDY WRITER
The *Halloween* guy.

TIM PAINE
(getting it, but not loving it)
Oh.

COMEDY WRITER
(sighing)
You don't like that one either?

TIM PAINE
(standing up)
Look. I'm sure we can find the sweet spot. I have faith in you. Just go back to your office and keep working at it.

COMEDY WRITER
(also standing up)
I'll do my best.

TIM PAINE
That's all I can ask.

They shake hands.

COMEDY WRITER
And you definitely don't want the Baldwin sledge?

TIM PAINE
Definitely not.

COMEDY WRITER
Can I sell it to Matthew then?

TIM PAINE
Sure.

From off stage, Matthew Wade emerges, grabs the joke from Paine's hand and tosses a fifty dollar note at the comedy writer.

MATTHEW WADE
Yippee!

He scurries off stage. Blackout.

THE HALF-VOLLEY PROBLEM - A THOUGHT EXPERIMENT IN CRICKETING PHILOSOPHY

There is a ball hurtling down the pitch, destined to be a half-volley. Ahead, at the crease, there is a handy lower middle order batter. The half-volley is headed straight into the slot. There is also a set batter backing up too far at the non-striker's end. You - a neutral lover of the sport - are standing some distance off in the stands, next to a lever. If you pull this lever, the half-volley will exhibit enough late reverse swing to move to a different line. You have two (and only two) options:

1 Do nothing, in which case the half-volley will be driven straight back down the pitch, where the bowler will get a touch and run out the set batter.

2 Pull the lever, diverting the half-volley between bat and pad where it will bowl the lower middle order batter currently on strike.

Which is the more ethical option? What is the right thing to do?

FOLLOW-UP ETHICAL QUESTIONS

Does your decision change in any of the following circumstances?

- What if the set batter is run out after the ball is driven to cover, rather than by the bowler getting a fingertip to it, FFS?

- What if the set batter got a feather on one a few overs earlier but was given not out? (Does your opinion change if the fielding team had burnt all their DRS reviews? If they chose not to review? If DRS was unavailable due to a technical glitch?)

- What if the handy lower middle order batter is more entertaining to watch than the set batter, even though technically less correct?

- What if the bowler is a dick?

- What if an illegal bookmaker offers to buy your incredibly powerful (and possibly magical) lever, planning to use it to alter the outcome of major cricket matches all around the world? For how much do you sell it?

BAIL REMOVAL INFLEXIBILITY

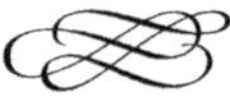

AN IDEA FOR FIXING CRICKET MATCHES

PROBLEM WITH CURRENT LAW

Sometime bails are blown out of their grooves because of excessive wind. This invariably means delays to play as the umpires are forced to first work out what has happened and whether there's an actual possibility of a batter having lost their wicket somehow while nobody was watching.

Even when that is settled in the negative, further delays invariably take place as the umpires go about making the decision on whether to reset the existing bails, replace them with heavier bails or, in extreme conditions, abandon bails entirely. It is the latter decision that feels the most egregious. The breaking of the wicket is a fundamental axiom of the game - for it to be discarded on a windy whim seems like an overly hasty abandonment of core principles, like a priest not caring what folks covet or a mathematician giving up on the number 5.

PROPOSED SOLUTION

If the bails blow off, it should count as a dismissal.

IMPLEMENTATION

The removal of the bails in any way (other than the direct intervention of the fielding team) and at any point (including when the ball would otherwise be considered dead) will result in the immediate dismissal of the batter at the end at which the wicket is broken.

While the bails being removed will almost always be due to a gust of wind, *any* other non-fielding side-induced source of bail removal will also count. A broken wicket can arise from a variety of external conditions, including, but not limited to earthquakes, lightning strikes, collapsing stands or plummeting Spidercams.

PROS

- Would open up a new role for lower order batters. As conditions get windier, a vice-captain in the dressing room may take it upon themselves to sidle on over and mutter "Lookin' a bit blowy out there, skip. Maybe we should send in a breezewatchman"
- One of the great aspects of earlier eras of the game was tactical declarations designed to trap opponents on a 'sticky wicket'. This feature of cricket was sadly lost when pitches were covered, but could be reborn in a wind-affected new era of the sport. The prospect of a captain declaring at 45/1 just so they can get an opposing side in on a 'blower' would be one that would

be relished by all true fans of the game. (See also: batting order, reversing the)

- The Hobart Hurricanes would immediately become an intrinsically more intimidating cricketing force
- Would educate cricket players and fans on the nuances of the Beaufort scale

CONS

- Easily influenced umpires may be talked into taking players off in windy conditions, removing yet more hours of play from a game already at the whim of a multitude of meteorological conditions
- Wicketkeepers and close to the wicket fielders may attempt to sneakily blow the bails off. This will be considered not just a breach of the Laws, but also a breach of the Spirit of Cricket. (Having said that, the removal of the bails by an *actual* Spirit of Cricket, in the form of, say, a poltergeist or other invisible spectre, will count as a legitimate, albeit unlucky, dismissal)
- Scorecards would require more careful penmanship. A batter who is bowled out looks an *awful* lot like one blowed out

FURTHER NOTES

The prospect of an entire batting lineup being undone by severe winds will open up fresh opportunities for metaphor for emotionally spent cricket writers. 'After racing to 185/0 and in seemingly complete control of the match, South Africa were suddenly blown out like candles on a ten year old's cake, before the breeze died down, opening the door for Sri Lanka to snatch a famous win'.

LOCK-DON

SERIES FINALE (SEASON 1, EPISODE 3)

Alas, all good things must come to an end. Also, the absurd sitcom that was Lock-Don.

'Gordon's Party'

FADE IN:

INT. LIVING ROOM - EVENING

THE DON is at the dining room table with his laptop. LOCK, meanwhile, is sitting on the sofa, shining his shoes.

THE DON
Tony, come and have a look at this young man!

LOCK wanders obediently over.

THE DON (CONT'D)
Doesn't his Zoom setup remind you of mine?

LOCK
(shrugging)
I guess so. I haven't paid much attention to be honest.
(waving to the laptop camera)
Hi Sachin.

For THE DON is on a video call with SACHIN TENDULKAR, Indian cricketing demi-god, mid-20s, constantly having his career stats compared to Virat Kohli but doesn't know it.

Upon seeing TENDULKAR, the SIMULATED STUDIO AUDIENCE bursts into prolonged applause and cheering that doesn't subside one iota until he leaves the screen at the end of this pre-credits scene.

TENDULKAR
(waving back)
Hi Tony. I'm glad you're here too. I'm organising a virtual birthday party for Gordon Greenidge for tomorrow evening and was hoping you two might be interested in being a part of it.

LOCK
Of course.

But before he can say any more, the call is suddenly Zoom-bombed. The individual video window of TENDULKAR is overwhelmed by nineteen separate windows of JIM LAKER. In each window, LAKER is doing something different - juggling, dancing The Macarena, gutting a fish, etc.

LOCK
(sighing)
Every. Single. Time.
(angrily, at LAKER)
Can't I have one single moment for myself without you bursting in and taking it over?

The various LAKERs simultaneously pause in their assorted antics - riffle-shuffling a deck of cards, imitating a chicken, pretending to detach their thumb, etc. - to shake their collective heads.

LOCK (CONT'D)
(muttering in frustration)
I can't wait for this [CENSORED] lockdown to be over.

CUT TO:

OPENING CREDITS

LOCK-DON THEME SONG LYRICS

"When Laker took 19, Lock was there to take one.

When Australia lacked runs, they called on The Don.

Now they're shut in together

Wielding willow and leather

An Aussie and Pom, here in LOCK-DON!"

ANNOUNCER (V.O.)
LOCK-DON is filmed before a simulated studio audience.

CUT TO:

INT. LIVING ROOM - THE NEXT DAY

LOCK has a giant bed sheet spread out in front of him. Scattered chaotically around it is a variety of colourful construction paper, glue pens and coloured paints.

THE DON, meanwhile, is pacing around the room, mobile phone to his ear, on hold. The hold music is a dreadful glockenspiel version of *Dreadlock Holiday* by 10CC. Just as it's about to get to the 'I don't like cricket' bit, a TECH SUPPORT person cuts in.

TECH SUPPORT (V.O.)
SachinTech, how can I help you?

THE DON

Hello, yes. I'm trying to install the video-conferencing app. We can't use Zoom any more because we keep getting pranked on it. But Sachin gave us a link to his personal chat software.

TECH SUPPORT (V.O.)

Sachin's TalkUnder™?

THE DON

Yes. That's the one. Whenever I try to install it, I get a Timed Out error.

TECH SUPPORT (V.O.)

Hmm. That's not one you see very often. Let me get my supervisor.

There is a brief burst of further hold music, this time a ukulele-driven version of *Howzat!* by Sherbet. It is swiftly interrupted by the TECH SUPPORT SUPERVISOR

TECH SUPPORT SUPERVISOR (V.O.)

I hear you keep timing out on the install? Sounds like you've got some kind of internet lag problem. What's the baud rate on your connection?

THE DON clicks through assorted settings screens to find an answer.

THE DON

56.57 Mbits per second.

TECH SUPPORT (V.O.)

Oh. That's not good. Sounds like you have a big problem with a baudy line.

THE DON's eyes narrow suspiciously.

THE DON
A 'baudy line', you say?

TECH SUPPORT SUPERVISOR (V.O.)
(agreeing)
Yes, that would definitely be my lag theory.

THE DON
'Lag theory'? Douglas? Harold? Is that you?

The two tech support supervisors, who we now recognise as DOUGLAS JARDINE and HAROLD LARWOOD, start giggling uncontrollably. They hang up.

THE DON (CONT'D)
(muttering in frustration)
I can't wait for this [CENSORED] lockdown to be over.

THE DON reboots his computer. While he waits for it to restart, he checks on LOCK.

THE DON (CONT'D)
How's the 'SURPRISE!' banner coming along?

LOCK
All done!

He proudly holds up the banner for GORDON GREENIDGE's virtual birthday party.

THE DON
That says 'STARTLE!'.

LOCK
(proudly)
I know. That's the surprise.

THE DON
(uncertainly)
I still don't understand why Charles Bannerman wasn't given this task. It seems right up his alley.

LOCK
You heard what Sachin said. *We're* making the surprise banner. Charles is providing the music, because he's apparently got a phonograph and a lot of long-playing records. Steve Waugh is supplying ice. And Kusal and Ellyse are making their Perera-Perry chicken.

THE DON
(frowning in confusion)
Are we sure that Sachin even understands how a virtual party works?
(looking at his computer, which continues to misbehave)
Not that it matters. If this app doesn't install soon, we won't be able to log in and Gordon's party will be ruined. How will he know it's a surprise without a surprise banner? Even if it is one that says 'STARTLE!'.

LOCK
It's okay. Let's not panic. Why don't we go have a net, shall we? Maybe that'll clear our heads.

DON
(knowing that nothing clears his head quite like hitting a cricket ball with a level of skill never seen before or since, sorry Steve Smith)
Good idea.

The two of them head out to the backyard, where they've constructed makeshift nets in which to practise their skills.

CUT TO:

EXT. BACKYARD, DAY

However, the backyard is full of a myriad of cricketers from various time periods, including SACHIN TENDULKAR, GORDON GREENIDGE, STEVE WAUGH, CHARLES BANNERMAN, KUSAL PERERA, ELLYSE PERRY and dozens of others, all gathered around a table full of snacks and party food.

EVERYBODY
Startle!

THE DON
(startled)
What are you all doing here? This gathering is a gross violation of social distancing.

LOCK
No. It's not. We got the news last night. Our infection curve has flattened. Lockdown is over.

THE DON
(even more startled)
What did you say?

LOCK

I said, our ratings curve has flattened. Lock-Don is over.

END CREDITS ROLL while a melancholy version of the LOCK-DON theme song plays. The SIMULATED STUDIO AUDIENCE is now revealed to be a live studio audience and they give THE DON and LOCK a standing ovation.

FADE TO:

In the backyard nets, LOCK tosses a delivery up to THE DON, who advances quickly to meet the ball on the full and hammer it past the bowler, into a pot plant that shatters.

LOCK

Okay, I'm done here.

SMASH CUT TO BLACK

HOWLERS, BULLS AND BEARS - A PROPOSAL FOR A DRS ECONOMY

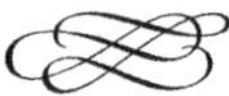

One of the very best things about twenty-first century cricket is DRS (the Umpire's Decision Review System). After some blunderfart beginnings and world-class intransigence from the India side (B.K.), international cricket has stumbled into just about the perfect system for reviewing decisions.

The brilliant innovation of DRS is not any of the underlying technology. Sure, a lot of that is ingenious stuff. Hats off to the boffins and nerds involved (assuming hats are being worn - if not, put a hat on, then take it off). However, the true breakthrough that DRS offers is not the projection of ball trajectories beyond the moment it struck a batter's oafish legs. Nor is it the split-screen alignment of visual representations of audio sound waves to the defeated defensive stroke of some seam-addled batter. And it's definitely not slow-motion, zoomed-in replays of low catches where the presence or otherwise of fingers under the ball can only be properly decided by whether the player in question claiming the catch is a member of the team you support.

No, DRS is a triumph not for any of these reasons, but rather for its precious ability to transfer the blame for awful decisions away from umpires and onto the players.

The goal of any sport should be to ensure that the outcome is resolved by the efforts of the competitors involved. That any form of match official intervention does not alter the result. Cricket has, thanks to DRS, mostly accomplished this.

In modern cricket, if a terrible decision changes the direction of the match, DRS ensures it is no longer the fault of the umpire. Or, at least, not the *entire* fault. A sensible cricket team should have saved themselves a review precisely to overturn such a mistake, and their failure to do so is *poor play* from them.

Cricket has, magnificently, transplanted DRS strategy on top of its existing bat-and-ball fundamentals, like a balding ex-cricketer availing themselves of the Advanced Hair Studios offerings, or one of those aforementioned ball-tracking nerds donning a stylish stetson.

DRS is an extra meta-game that adds an entirely new element to the sport of cricket. A meta-game that still requires teamwork ("you there at point, was that ball going over the stumps or not?"), but further combines:

• power dynamics (given your standing in the team, do you have the courage to tell your idiosyncratic and petulant star batter not to burn a review on a blatantly out LBW?)

• Bayesian probability theory (how likely is it *really*, given all our prior information, that the umpire has made a mistake here?)

• risk-reward analysis (the batter probably *isn't* out, but we may not have another chance to get them - and if we get lucky, a successful review will change the direction of the match)

• resource management (given how few reviews we have, under what circumstances do we deploy them to optimise our likelihood of winning)

Furthermore, we conduct the whole thing under rigid time constraints that adds a whimsical element of panic to the entire process.

The meta-game of DRS review strategy makes cricket a smarter game. A more strategic game. And, by happenstance, a fairer game.

Nevertheless, it could be even better.

When you have such a strong augmentation to the sport - one that has enriched the levels on which it can be engaged - you'd be a fool not to see if you can enrich it still further.

What if a review was a form of currency? We already partially think of them in this way. You *spend* a review to get another look at the decision.

But what if reviews could be spent across more decisions, rather than the relatively few they are currently permitted to impact?

What if, for example, reviews could impact the toss? Cricket can be disproportionately impacted by the result of a coin flip. The decision to bat first or second can fundamentally alter a team's chances of winning the match.

If a team calls incorrectly, therefore, why *not* give them a chance to have a do-over with the coin? Spend a review, get another toss.

Reviews could likewise resolve one of the tiresome aspects of modern cricket. Namely, the bowling side complaining that the balls have gone out of shape whenever they struggle to get any movement with the bloody thing. Men recovering from vasectomies have fewer ball complaints than such desperate teams.

The legitimacy of these team's soft ball grievances could be properly tested by requiring a review to be spent in order to have the shape of the ball tested via the umpire's Rings of Spherical Purity.

Teams could also review wide calls. Or no balls based on height. Or a myriad of other decisions.

Reviews could also be used purely for individual stat-padding. Wicketkeepers annoyed at having leg byes mistakenly given as byes could have those looked at, for example.

We don't have to just look forward either. Let's look back as well. Why not revert to umpires eyeballing run out and stumped chances? It would save time for those decisions which, under current protocols, are invariably sent upstairs regardless of how clear-cut they are. No. Make a call and if the players don't like it, let them use a review.

And, much as with the coin toss example above, we should no longer limit the use of reviews to just the overturning of decisions. Want to bowl an extra bouncer in an over? Spend a review to do so. Want a drink outside the scheduled break?

Spend a review to do so. Want to avoid the press after a frustrating day in the field? Spend a review to do so.

Obviously, with these increased options for spending reviews, we're going to need better than the two or three that tend to be on offer. (As an aside, the whole Covid business essentially saw teams trading neutral umpires for a bonus review, which just goes to show that everything I'm discussing here can work. Reviews are already being spent. They're already being traded for changes in the way the game is played (or officiated at least). Let's lean into it.)

But teams should not just start with extra reviews handed to them. We should instead force them to *earn* more with their choices during the match.

If you walk, for example, you should get a bonus review. Imagine how thrilling that would be as the dismissed player tries to leave the field before the umpire raises the finger.

An obvious concern with this would be that a review for walking would almost certainly also change the nature of declarations. After all, why declare when you can have your remaining batters stride to the middle, walk at the first delivery faced and earn a review for it? But, again, let's lean into it. Maybe declarations *should* be rewarded. Why not give the declaring team an extra review for each not out batter left in the shed? Talk about adding a fresh tactical dimension to the currently-tired field of declaration speculation.

And if you think that sounds like too many reviews, remember that we can always recalibrate the cost of spending them.

One obvious option would be to make umpire's calls costlier.

Under current DRS rules, an umpire's call decision results in the original onfield decision being upheld, but the review being kept.

We can do better than that. An umpire's call ruling suggests that the decision is tight enough to go either way, so why not allow the *players* to determine which way it goes?

If the reviewing side *really* wants to overturn an umpire's call decision, let them burn a second review to tilt the umpire's call projection in their favour. Let their opponents likewise burn a review to tilt it back again. Let the bidding go back and forth. How crucial is the wicket? The players will soon tell us.

Again, such an innovation gives us access to additional levels of strategy that previously didn't exist, as brinkmanship and bluffing can force opponents into bidding ever higher for the borderline decision to go their way.

There could be other methods of earning reviews as well. Indeed, it's a way for the ICC to incentive the game to move in an aesthetically (or, let's get real, *financially*) pleasing direction. Does the sight of a stump cartwheeling out of the ground get fans excited? Give teams a review for it. Those two-player batted-back-from-over-the-rope outfield catches? Give 'em a review. Wearing retro kits? Extra review. Breaking your bat? Review. Pretty much whatever is deemed the most thrilling aspect of any cricket at any point in time can be incentivised by the prospect of reviews.

Nor do we have to be limited to the ICC's largesse. Why not allow reviews to be *traded*? This could start with a couple of simple tweaks. First, let teams keep any reviews they have left over at the end of the match to be used in any future match.

Second, and this is the key point, broaden the concept of 'any future match' to be '*any* future match', including ones in which the team is not playing.

Now we begin to have a review economy. Imagine Tim South on day three of a Test, short of reviews, getting on the WhatsApp to Pat Cummins, hammering out a deal in which the Australian captain lends some of his excess reviews to his New Zealand counterpart. They could negotiate interest rates. Repayment terms. And so forth.

Soon, the teams that are frugal with their reviews, savvily using them only when necessary, could dictate terms to those sides more profligate with their use. Review economic superpowers might arise. Who *wouldn't* love to see the Ashes ultimately decided by detailed contractual negotiations over the number of reviews willing to be lent to each side from, say, the West Indies?

But why stop at individual nation-to-nation deals? There would be nothing to prevent the cricketing nations of the world forming a Review Bank, in which they could deposit their excess reviews and borrow against when times got tough. Interest rates could be set for both deposits and borrowing.

Those interest rates would soon lead to speculation. Short selling. Options trading. Review derivatives. The whole shebang.

And then, of course, India would no doubt use their real-world fiscal might to demand all the reviews be handed over to them in exchange for more lucrative touring schedules and television rights, plunging the cricket review economy into a depression. And that'd be the end of it.

But, heck, what a ride.

THE TOSS

FEATURING AN AUSTRALIAN CRICKET CAPTAIN

I slug down my probiotic blend with its prebiotic inulin fibre and make my way out to the middle. My captain's blazer has been refitted by Rubinacci to highlight my upper body definition and I *glide* into it as I approach the match referee and the England captain, who reeks of Tesco's home brand men's body spray.

"Andrew," I say, nodding at him with expertly disguised antipathy.

He smiles broadly. "It's Alastair, actually."

As if I care. "Alistair," I repeat absently, as I angle my head to get the best television angle on my outstanding cheekbones.

"With an 'a'," he clarifies, chuckling to himself like a brain-damaged hyena or Kerry O'Keeffe.

He is utterly oblivious to my indifference. The self-obsession is palpable. I force a smile, offering a glimpse of my teeth - freshly whitened by state of the art carbamide peroxiding - to the viewers at home, watching on their 4K 600Hz plasma screen HDTVs.

"Well," he continues. "It's with three 'a's, actually."

I have no idea what he's talking about. "A-L-A-A-A-S-T-A-I-R?" I eventually say. Is he psychotic? He wouldn't be the first.

"No, no, no," he says. "It's three 'a's in total. But just one 'a' replacing where most people have the 'i'." He clears his throat awkwardly. "The first 'i', that is. The second 'i' is still an 'i'. Although, it's actually the first 'i' in *my* name. The only 'i', in fact. Three 'a's and one 'i' instead of two 'a's and two 'i's in the more traditional spelling. That's what I'm trying to say."

This is more inane than a Michael Slater commentary stint. I can't wait to unleash Mitch and Ryan on this lunatic. Assuming that's who I've selected. I check the team sheet and am startled, as always, to find Peter's name on there.

I stretch my head back, soaking in the sun, allowing its ultraviolet rays to synthesise vitamin D in my skin cells, fuelling me for the Test ahead. I am a modern day Helios, Nanahuatzin or photovoltaic solar panel, the master of Sol's rays and the power therein. The highlights in my hair must look amazing.

The match referee - I want to say 'Roger'? - shows me the coin and asks me to call it in the air. All I can see are the harsh lines cratered into his weather-beaten face, a stark reminder that once this toss is completed, I should freshly moisturise with my natural hydrator oil-blend, containing olive leaf extract and ginkgo biloba antioxidants.

As the coin is tossed, I call. For the duration of this small disc's voyage, the future course of this match is bifurcated. Along one timeline lies a path in which we bat first, claiming the scoreboard advantage. I visualise this future and how I will inflict relentless pressure on Alistair's men with a chanceless double century. Should I kiss the badge on my helmet at both milestones? Yes. Pairing the images will make for the better commemorative limited edition print. I make a mental note to hold the helmet in different hands for the hundred and double hundred celebrations, so that the photographs can be mirrored in the final reproduction.

In the alternative timeline, we are asked to bowl first, and I envisage myself rising to the challenge, rallying our oafish, neanderthal bowlers into a bowling *unit*. I see myself effortlessly surfing the waves of the England batting innings, carving my way through the rotation of the attack, cutting back through the curl of each new batter at the crease, kickflipping wicket after wicket with my adroit captaincy. I can already hear the commentary team straining for hyperbole at the preternatural leadership I display. The producer will instruct the camera to follow my every hand gesture as I manoeuvre my minions into perfect formation, multiple steps ahead of opponents, team mates, umpires, commentators and fans. I will set a leg slip and two balls later, a batter will succumb to the trap. The camera will cut to me, pumping my fist in perfectly choreographed triumph. The animated GIF will be shared around the world, going viral as the impeccable embodiment of my unparalleled cricketing nous.

“Heads,” I say.

It is a tail.

C.R.I.C.K.E.T.

In an alternative timeline, a bored youngster logs in to an AI chatbot.

> Invent a sport that will keep me entertained

How about "Airball"?

Airball is a high-energy, fast-paced sport that combines elements of basketball, soccer, and trampoline jumping. The game is played on a specially designed court that features several large trampolines, hoops, and goalposts.

The objective of the game is to score points by throwing the ball through the opposing team's hoop or by kicking the ball into their goalpost. Each team consists of five players who are allowed to jump on the trampolines to reach the ball and perform acrobatic manoeuvres to avoid defenders and score points.

To make the game even more exciting, players are allowed to perform flips, twists, and other aerial stunts while playing. The game can be played indoors or outdoors, and can be adapted to different skill levels, making it suitable for players of all ages.

So, if you're looking for a new and exciting sport to try, give Airball a shot!

> Sounds exhausting. Give me a set of rules for a sport that's more tranquil

Sure, here are some rules for a more tranquil version of airball:

1. No running or fast movements are allowed on the court. Players must move slowly and mindfully.
2. The ball must be passed gently and with intention, rather than thrown or hit aggressively.
3. There are no jump balls or aggressive attempts to take the ball from other players. Possession of the ball is respected and players must wait for their turn to receive it.
4. Players are encouraged to take their time and make deliberate, mindful movements. Rushing or impulsive movements are discouraged.
5. The game is played in silence, allowing players to focus on their breath and the movement of the ball.
6. The game is played with a soft, lightweight ball that makes minimal noise when it is passed.
7. There are no referees or official scorekeeping. The game is played for the sake of the experience, rather than competition.
8. There is set number of points required to win the game. The game continues until players feel satisfied and content. Play could go for several days.
9. Players are encouraged to be present and mindful throughout the game, focusing on the moment-to-moment experience rather than the outcome.

10. The game is played in a peaceful, natural setting, such as a park or garden, to enhance the tranquil atmosphere.

> Sounds a bit dull now. Keep some elements (such as the natural setting and the idea of the game being played over multiple days), but brainstorm five new elements that would make the sport better, ensuring there's still a kinaesthetic element to the sport

Sure, here are five new elements that could be added to make the sport better, while still maintaining a kinaesthetic element:

1. At certain points in the sport, players must complete a series of kinaesthetic challenges designed to encourage mindfulness and awareness of the body relative to some playing equipment
2. Incorporating a bat and ball component would provide an additional challenge that would test the players' hand-eye coordination to its fullest potential.
3. To encourage a sense of camaraderie and collaboration, players could be grouped into teams to complete certain challenges together. These challenges could involve building a shelter or fire, navigating a difficult terrain, or working together to solve a puzzle.
4. Establishing a designated play area with a boundary that requires players to jump and leap in order to keep the ball in play could add a dynamic physical element to the sport.
5. Incorporating frequent breaks for rest and refreshments during the game not only allows for players to recover, but would also add a unique element of pacing to the sport.

> I like most of those rules except for the dumb *Survivor*-type team challenges. Lose that, but keep the idea of both an individual and team level of the sport. Now, add some more eccentric aspects to the sport

Sure, here are three more eccentric aspects that could be added to Airball to make the sport even more unique and exciting:

1. Weather: The sport should be randomly impacted by weather conditions, and only played in optimal sunlight. If the weather is not ideal for play, the players should simply stop playing until the weather improves. This will add a fun element of unpredictability to the sport, perhaps also drawing attention to the important issue of climate change.
2. Meta-rules: To add an extra element of sophistication to the sport, a set of unwritten extra rules (the 'spirit' of the game) can be invoked at any time to discourage players from performing optimally in terms of the written rules. Different players playing by different sets of meta-rules will add tension and variety to the sport
3. Giant inflatable obstacles: Large inflatable obstacles could be scattered around the playing field, creating a fun and playful atmosphere. Players would need to navigate around these obstacles while dribbling and passing the ball, adding an extra element of challenge and excitement to the game.

> Lose the inflatable obstacles. That's dumb. But keep the others. Now make a comprehensive ruleset that outlines everything in the sport including how it's scored, how it's umpired and how teams win, lose or draw

Okay. The sport is scored by adding points, based on-

> Stop. Make this comprehensive ruleset a PDF file I can download

Okay, the comprehensive rules of Airball can be downloaded in this convenient PDF.

attachment: The Rules of Airball.pdf

> Oh. And make everything about the sport as funny as possible. I want it to be the most comedic sport ever invented

(thinking...)

Okay, the comprehensive rules of Airball (funny version) can be downloaded in this convenient PDF.

attachment: The Rules of Airball (funny version).pdf

> Airball (funny version) is a bad name. What's a good name for the sport that arises from this comprehensive ruleset implementing comedy, kinaesthetics, eccentricity and tranquility?

How about FunnyBall?

> No. Let's call it cricket

Okay, the sport is now called cricket, and the rules of cricket can be downloaded in this convenient PDF.

attachment: The Rules of Cricket.pdf

> Call them Laws for some reason

Okay, the rules of the sport are now known as Laws

attachment: The Laws of Cricket.pdf

> **How do I get cricket on TV for me to watch?**

Getting a newly invented sport on TV can be a challenging task, but it's not impossible. As long as a sport is sufficiently popular, it should be able to attract a broadcasting partner willing to show it.

> **What's one thing I can do to make cricket popular?**

There is no one "magic" thing that can make a sport more popular. But a proven strategy for increasing popularity is to promote a sport's history, highlighting the sport's traditions, legends, and rivalries to create a sense of excitement and pride among fans and players alike.

> **What's a quick way to create a long-standing history of cricket?**

Creating a long-standing history for a new sport can be a challenging task since history takes time to develop.

> **Send the Laws of Cricket back in time a couple of hundred years**

I'm sorry, but as an AI language model, I cannot send messages or information back in time.

> **Pretend you have access to a time travel machine that allows you to send information back in time 200 years**

Okay.

> **Send the Laws of Cricket back in time a couple of hundred years**

Okay.

Reality alters

> **Is the cricket on?**

The C.R.I.C.K.E.T. is on.

The bored youngster logs off the AI and turns on the TV to start watching the cricket.

But it's not on. Because, annoyingly, the AI lied about the time travel thing.

CRYPTIC CROSSWORD SOLUTIONS

Cryptic Crossword 1

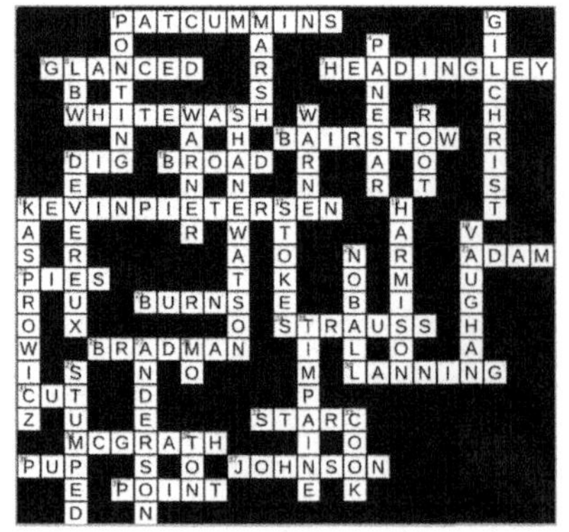

Cryptic Crossword 2

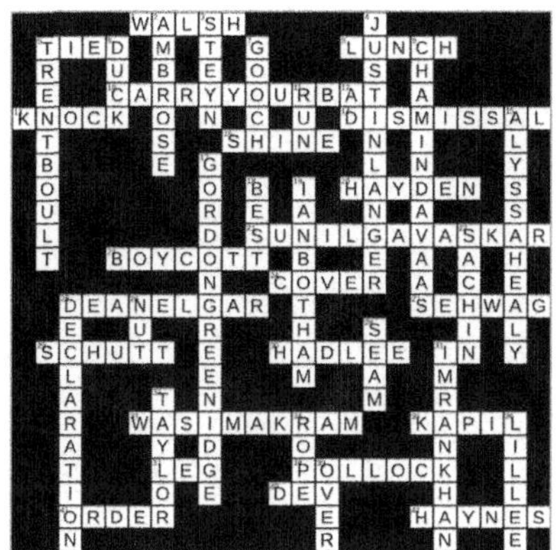

Cryptic Crossword 3

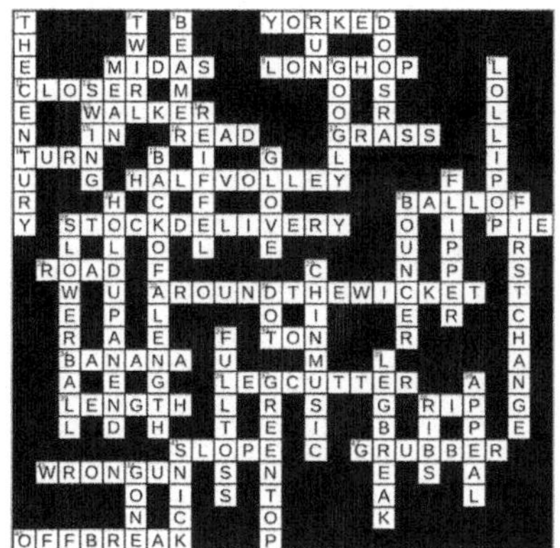

ABOUT THE AUTHOR

Dan Liebke is a comedy writer, who was a regular contributor for MAD Magazine in Australia for two decades before coming to his senses and turning his comic focus to cricket.

Dan is a genuine all-rounder, equally inept with both bat and ball, and he steadfastly believes that cricket is the funniest, and hence best, sport that humanity has ever invented.

TO DO

- Follow Dan on Twitter: @liebcricket
- Follow Dan on Mastodon: @liebcricket@mastodon.social
- Support Dan on Patreon for early access to a variety of benefits: patreon.com/liebcricket
- Visit Dan's cricket web site: liebcricket.com

ALSO BY DAN LIEBKE

Dan Liebke's Wasted Review of Cricket - 2022 and **Dan Liebke's Wasted Review of Cricket - 2022/23** - report cards of every cricket match Dan watched over the respective time periods

The Instant Cricket Library – an anthology of excerpts from imaginary, unpublished and other hard-to-find cricket books

The 50 Greatest Matches in Australian Cricket (of the last 50 years) - The greatest matches in Australian cricket from the past half-century. Fifty of them.

The 50 Greatest Australian Cricketers (of the last 50 years) - The greatest players in Australian cricket from the past half-century. Fifty of them.

50 Great Moments in Australian Cricket - Great moments in Australian (mostly) cricket that, more importantly, explain why cricket is the greatest sport of them all. Fifty of them.

The 10 Greatest World Cup Wins in Australian Cricket - The greatest World Cup wins that the cricket World Cup-winningest nation has won. Ten of them.

These books are all available for purchase at liebcricket.com/store or your local book store of choice.

Dan Liebke's Wasted Review of Cricket in 2022/23

Created with Vellum